MARKETING & PROMOTION FOR CRAFTS

- An essential guide to selling for all makers.

- Practical and authoritative advice from an experienced exhibition organiser, gallery owner and marketing consultant.

- What to do and, equally important, what not to do, to improve your image, your marketing skills and your public relations.

- How to set up and run your own exhibitions successfully.

- Covers: marketing, sales opportunities, exhibition organising, approaching the media, finance, creating a customer base, public relations, etc.

Betty Norbury is well-known in the world of fine woodworking and is a prolific writer on the subject for trade journals. She organises and manages numerous exhibitions of leading craftsmen and runs the White Knight Gallery which specifically markets her husband's work. (Ian Norbury is considered to be one of the country's foremost wood sculptors.) She is a marketing consultant and advisor to professional makers.

MARKETING

&

PROMOTION

FOR CRAFTS

Betty Norbury

STOBART DAVIES

HERTFORD

British Library Cataloguing in Publication Data.
A catalogue record for this book is available from the British Library.

ISBN 0–85442–062–2

Published 1995 by Stobart Davies Ltd, Priory House, Priory Street, Hertford SG14 1RN.
Set in 10 on 14 pt Bookman by Ann Buchan (Typesetters) Shepperton.
Printed by BPC Wheatons Ltd, Exeter.

For Ian

'. . . subtle accumulation of nuances,
a hundred things done a little better, . . .'

Henry Kissinger

By the same author
British Craftsmanship in Wood

Contents

	Introduction	9
CHAPTER 1	The Market Place	11
CHAPTER 2	Motivation & Goal Setting	16
CHAPTER 3	You	22
CHAPTER 4	Your Work	28
CHAPTER 5	Presentation	32
CHAPTER 6	Pricing Your Work	38
CHAPTER 7	Commission	43
CHAPTER 8	Managing Your Money	47
CHAPTER 9	Research	55
CHAPTER 10	Lists & Indexes	62
CHAPTER 11	Communication	68
CHAPTER 12	Sales Opportunities	81
CHAPTER 13	Organizing Your Own Exhibitions	93
CHAPTER 14	The Media	108
CHAPTER 15	Public Relations	120
	Bibliography	125

Introduction

To succeed as a craftsman it is not enough to be good at your work, in fact when one looks around at the work that is acclaimed as outstanding, sometimes it is easy to feel that quality is irrelevant to success. This point does, in fact, illustrate very well that, indeed, the work is not enough. The other three important factors are presentation, marketing and promotion. You may feel that the quality of the work should be enough and that everyone should know who you are and where you live. Why are they not beating a path to your door? Which of you when attending exhibitions, reading articles, and listening to tales of mouthwatering commissions have not said 'I could do that. Why didn't they ask me?' The answer is usually very simply – that they did not know about you. As difficult as it is to accept, and even more difficult to change, you have got to be a mixture of craftsman, salesman, public relations officer and packager. To be thought of by the people promoting crafts, you have to maintain a high profile and do the work they find acceptable or, if that is too unpalatable, you must promote and market your own work.

Working for yourself in the field of crafts and making a good living is no easy task and it is compounded by the perceived low professional position that the craftsman occupies. Whilst is is not true of all countries, in the U.K. craft is generally considered a second class occupation, and it is a very difficult image to shrug off. There are a few who have managed to elevate their work and their standing above their contemporaries in the trade, but it is still possible to stop hundreds of people in the street and ask for the name of a designer/craftsman or maker and they will not know what you are talking about. They may know a local restorer or a local cabinet maker, but they would also give you the name of the local carpenter just as readily. It is only those people who have been exposed to first class craftsmanship who are able to differentiate between a chippie and a furniture maker, and whilst this is a growing minority, it is still a very small percentage of the population.

The very word 'craft' to the vast majority of the population means macrame hanging baskets, pottery animals, knitted cushion covers, mug trees, etc., knocked out in their hundreds, some of it cheaply imported, and sold at the growing number of craft fairs up and down the country. The word has been degenerated and it now encompasses the work of our top craftsmen and the people selling dried leaves and chocolates in the same breath.

So how can you elevate your standing in the community and become a maker who is respected and employed in worthwhile and satisfactory work? One that will still be working in his chosen field in twelve months' time.

In this book it has been my intention to lay out all the positive and constructive things that you can do to promote and market your work and to maximise your potential to encourage success in whatever way you would wish to measure that commodity. It is not intended as a factual guide on accounting, tax, etc. for running a small business. For those in need of such information there are many excellent books on the market which deal purely with management and general business aspects of company control.

On the contentious issue of gender, throughout the text I have deliberately refrained from using craftsmen/women, his/her, etc., in favour of adopting the single male gender. I apologise in advance if this causes the reader any irritation or offence.

In terms of the information and advice offered in this book, I hope that you will read it and use it in the spirit in which it is written. Nothing would give me greater joy than to see the crafts attract and maintain a higher and more respected profile. It is one of my great ambitions that when seeking a substantial purchase the potential buyer does not ask himself 'Antique or mass produced?' but rather 'Antique, mass produced, or craftsman made?' and that he will know where to go to choose or commission.

I wish you success.

CHAPTER ONE

The Market Place

It is necessary that you understand some of the basic aspects of the market place in which you will need to place your work to sell it. Understanding what the competition is, what is influencing choice and the way the public perceive crafts will give you some forewarning of what you are up against. In this way you are able to meet the challenge head on and work either within the perceived parameters or work at breaking the mould. The decisions will be yours and you will make them with your eyes wide open.

Competition will come mainly from four sources: your contemporaries, the new trend for products that look handmade, high quality mass produced work and antiques.

Unless you make something that is easily copied, as do woodturners and potters for instance, then competition from your contemporaries is not really a great problem, contemporary craftsmen tend to have a style that is, generally speaking, all their own and the customer will usually prefer one style to another. The area where competition from other craftsmen may affect you more noticeably is if you make reproductions. There are many craftsmen using tried and tested designs of the old masters and here I feel you will only gain the edge by your work being seen in the right places and being better in every aspect than that of your competitor.

There is also a more unusual aspect of competition now by the encroachment of mass producers into what has always been deemed to be the province of the craftsman. Decoy ducks perhaps illustrate this point best; as they have become a fashionable, decorative item in the home, so they have become more and more available. Whilst you can still buy one hand made by a craftsman for many hundreds of pounds, you can also buy a cheap one in a chain store for fifty. You can see evidence of this, not usually as extreme as this example, generally in the more trendy shops, where the buyer is seeking a 'less mass produced' item. This may not be competition as such, more a trivialisation of the aesthetics of the product, but it cannot be denied that a percentage of the people who buy the mass produced item would purchase the craftsman-made original if there were no option. Could it be a step in the right direction that people are seeking a 'less mass produced' product that looks handmade even if many of them are not able or prepared to pay the extra cost involved?

The real competition comes from the next two sources. First, high quality mass produced work. For example, in the case of furniture, not mass produced chipboard units, but rather first class furniture produced by companies such as Ercol in the United Kingdom. Their furniture is well designed, beautifully produced and excellently marketed. If you were to visit their factory they would proudly show you how their furniture has been designed for the growing family, starting with the newly-weds of either today, ten years ago or fifty years ago. The furniture can be purchased one piece at a time, and can be added to at will; today's sideboard will match the table and chairs bought five or even ten years ago. It is timeless and yet they continue to add contemporary designs to the range that complement existing pieces. In the manufacturing process the work that can be done on machines is done on machines, but that which needs the hand or the eye is still done that way. They are marketing their work in every high street in every town in the U.K. and there is even now a lively market for second-hand Ercol. My parents' Ercol has been in their home for as long as I can remember, being added to or changed for the current design, and it always sits well together. They, along with other Ercol clients, have become customers for life. When they add or update it will be Ercol, it is the same as their neighbours' but with an element of individual choice. They are only one example; this competition exists for every field of crafts: ceramics, textiles, etc., and is impossible for the craftsman to match and I feel that perhaps he shouldn't even try, but it is there.

Then there are antiques. This is perhaps the biggest hurdle in the sales race, one you must be aware of and take in your stride, not because of the direct competition, because there is none with antiques, but because of the 'investment factor' and the '"they don't make it like this anymore" brigade'. Most people would consider antiques to be an investment; when one buys an antique the money is still in the bank, so to speak. This would also apply to some more recent second-hand pieces ('antique' meaning at least 100 years' old). There are a great many shops now selling artifacts from the period that would fall into the second-hand description and there is no doubt that one can resell some of these pieces from as recent as the 30's and 40's period for more than one paid for them say five years ago. This is a certainty, the older or more collectable the piece the greater the demand, the more ready the sale, the greater the investment. When one buys a new piece from a designer/craftsman it is money out of the bank, except if one is buying the work of a few notable exceptions and even this is at the moment still a gamble. Not for ten or fifteen years will you know for certain that the craftsman's work is collectable and definitely an investment. One needs only to look at the escalating prices now being paid for

'Arts and Crafts Movement' pieces that twenty years ago were sold for a song in the auction rooms, sometimes not even recognised. Good antiques are also less expensive than the contemporary equivalent, they have a track record of acceptability in taste. Most people are unadventurous in the way they furnish their homes. An astute business man in the retail furniture and decor trade, once told me, 'Customers want the same as their neighbour's, but with more cherries'. If they buy a piece of Georgian furniture, their taste is not in question, their friends and their enemies accept that they have spent x on the piece, and will even be impressed, envious, what you will, but if they buy a piece of designer-made furniture of the very best quality they are putting their taste on the line. They may even have to explain to their friends who the maker is, whereas Chippendale is a household name. Their friends may be impressed or they may think they are mad. By patronising a craftsman they have taken two gambles, a) with their money, and b) with their standing with their friends. Don't run away with the idea that all people are the same, they are not, but there is a good sound basis for this belief or there would not be so many antique and second- hand shops about, nor such a huge demand for reproduction. Take heart, there are also the strong-minded who know what they like and don't give a fig what others think and enjoy all aspects of buying from an individual designer/craftsman.

Whether we like it or not, antiques, or should I say the exponents of antiques, have greatly influenced the vast majority of the buying public. Programmes about antiques appear on our televisions and can be heard on the radio at least once a week, whereas crafts take an extreme back seat, being given air time once or twice a year, if that. Now and again a craftsman is featured on local television or radio, but the coverage has no comparison. For reasons best known to the presenters of these programmes they then tell us that 'they don't make it like this any more; there is no craftsmanship these days', and the damage is done – if it is on the television, it must be so – what a shame all the craftsmen have died out. It isn't true, you and I both know it isn't true. We have to stand up and be counted, but it is very difficult to shout louder than the media, to get the media to listen, or to persuade them to give us air time as well.

Craft fairs and markets also influence the perception the general public have about crafts. It is my opinion that the general run of craft markets reduces crafts to cheap nick-nacks; the majority of work offered can be of a amateurish quality, poorly conceived, poorly worked and poorly displayed. The odd, genuine, excellent example of craft work is lost in the general mediocrity of the majority. I know that a great deal of effort must go into some of the work, and it is not my intention to denigrate these craftsmen, rather to encourage a selection procedure for these events and perhaps give them a star rating, but one cannot deny the influence these have on the general public. Cheap jewellery, uninteresting turned wooden bowls, endless bags of pot pouri, indifferent knitted jumpers, etc. etc. These local fairs or markets influence both the craftsmen and the buyers in that the visitors expect crafts to be cheap and cheerful and accordingly the craftsmen reduce the standard of their work so that it can be sold for a lesser amount. This is not to say that there are not excellent craft fairs, there are, but they are so few and far between that it is the influence of the majority that prevails.

Local and national craft guilds can have a more encouraging influence in that some of them have a quality control and only admit members whose work they consider to have reached a certain standard. A selection of the work is usually shown once a year and on the whole a much more wholesome feeling is generated for crafts.

The Crafts Council has an influence in the market place, not only for the buying public and the craftsmen whom they select and promote but for the craftsmen who are refused entry into this auspicious group. It is a government-backed body which selects craftsmen and women from all fields of the crafts world, promote them, show their work, and generally give them help and encouragement. The selection procedure would appear to the outsider to be arbitrary, and not always based on fine craftsmanship as their Royal Charter would imply. Some of the bizarre work they show for astonishing prices alongside some of the most beautifully made work of a few of the top names in the field of contemporary makers/designers encourages the general public in their belief that indeed 'there are no craftsmen about any more and, even if there are, ordinary people could not possibly afford to buy their work'. The craftsmen who seek selection and are refused, feel rejected and inadequate, they are influenced in trying to emulate the work that is 'acceptable' in order to join those they consider to be the elite. It is very difficult both in theory and in practice to assure yourself and the small majority of the public that are aware and buy crafts that the Crafts Council does not represent *all* that is best in British crafts.

The prejudices are more difficult to define. The one that comes most readily to mind is the customer who thinks that it will not take long to plane a couple of bits of wood and fix them together, or mould a pot, or set a few stones into a piece of silver, and that it cannot possibly cost that much. This is in complete contrast to the prospective client who feels he cannot afford it because it is hand made and therefore, without knowing the cost, will not consider owning something craftsman made. Another section of the public will feel that if you can make it so can they – just a few new tools and some spare time, knock one of those up in no time! These reactions to crafts are, I feel, a direct result of all the influences mentioned previously and the fairly low profile maintained by crafts generally.

Crafts are not only for the very rich and the museums, nor are they cheap and cheerful baubles. They are readily available for all, they can be well designed and beautifully made by craftsmen who only want to work at making an excellent product for happy and satisfied customers. But how to bring the two together? How do you get your work out into this seemingly hostile market place and find your customers? How do you build such a reputation that eventually they do beat a path to your door?

CHAPTER TWO

Motivation and Goal Setting

What motivates us and the goals we set ourselves are closely intertwined. You may become a craftsman because that is what you have always wanted to do; the big drawback to this is that you are unsure how this occupation will pay the bills and allow you the lifestyle that you have set for yourself. Your motivation, therefore, is the fulfilling of a spiritual need, and the goal you have set yourself is to make it supply your material needs. Previously you may not have seen this objective as a target, but as a hurdle, but it is helpful to see these challenges as goals and then work your way towards them one step at a time.

It is always a good idea to question, from time to time, one's motivation for doing the things we are doing. It is an even better idea to question our motives before we set out on a given path. There are some motives given for being a craftsman which sound wonderful in theory, but which in real life can generate negative feelings if they have not been examined carefully and the pluses and the minuses measured against each other and accepted.

If you consider money to be the prime factor in making the choice to become a craftsman it has to be said that this would be a wrong career move. It is very rare for a craftsman to earn prodigious sums of money in their own lifetimes and to enjoy a jet-setting lifestyle by his or her own earning capacity. There are of course names that will spring readily to mind, more in the area of art and design than in that of craft, but compared to the many practitioners they are few and far between. It is not, however, impossible to earn either a modest, a reasonable or even a good living in the crafts, and the more you earn the easier it becomes to earn more. It is essential to begin by setting your wages at a reasonable level, commensurate with your ability and the time taken to complete given tasks. If you begin on this sound footing it is then possible, in fact essential, to increase your earning capacity along with your own abilities, efficiency, expertise and reputation.

The idea of becoming a craftsman in order to become famous would be based on a fallacy and one that is perpetuated within one's own profession. It is easy to believe that because we know who is at the top of our own specialised field that the general public are also au fait with the 'Big Names'. What I am saying is well illustrated in this quote from a copy of the 'Arts Review' dated January 93:

'A recent Artmart survey of a thousand people came up with some alarming findings.
They illustrate the difficulty of the task facing an art magazine like this one which is attempting to reach a wide audience. Only 11% had ever purchased an original oil painting, over half replying that cost was a deterrent. A further half of those surveyed buy their pictures at department stores. When asked to name any popular British artist 38% named Rolf Harris. The also-rans were Constable (23%), Tony Hart (18%), Turner (14%), Lowrie [sic] (12%), Beryl Cook (9%) and Francis Bacon (2%). . . . a total of 116%??'

I feel the point is well made in a field which is so much better catered for and participated in than are the crafts. If you are prepared to settle for being well known within your own field and working away at expanding your circle then so be it. But be aware that the competition is fierce and you will have to excel at what you do or buy a big trumpet, or even both.

Many people like to be masters of their own salvation, to feast or famine by their own abilities, and are attracted to the idea of being their own boss. There are so many different trades and professions in which you can do this so you must ask yourself whether or not the creative one is the answer to your own needs.

It may be that you are due to retire, or the children need less of your time and you are channelling your energy into crafts, because you feel it is something you can do and you prefer to work for yourself. This generally implies that you have another source of income to fall back on while you perfect your abilities, when things are quiet, or when other things demand your attention. There are few occupations other than the crafts more suited to this lifestyle.

It can appear idyllic when you see a small cottage with a workshop-cum-showroom attached to it, whilst on holiday in the summer. 'That's the life', you say – 'practising my crafts in the daytime, selling it to passers-by, galleries hearing about me and asking for my work, gardening for all our vegetables, sitting by roaring fires in the winter.' I'm almost sold on it myself! But you must consider this ideal realistically, weigh against this, the rain and the cold, the lack of visitors out of the tourist season, the work that will be involved in finding enough customers and a gallery to take your work, let alone every craftsman's ideal of gallery owners beating a path to your door.

To enjoy creating things has to be one of the best reasons. We read much of niche markets. Researching the market to discover where our place may be. Making a product especially to suit the market. In the field of creativity there is no gap in the market for you to find and fill. There is always a market for the new, top quality product. Faberge's eggs were not filling a marketing requirement, but a need of the craftsman to make them. They were a huge success and created their own market; more and more extravagant designs were commissioned and bought. This may be an extreme case, but you will come across more mundane examples of the originator creating his own market.

It follows, therefore, that you must make what you want, to a very high standard and believe that out there is someone who wishes to purchase it. If this were not the case all peoples' furnishings would by now be standardized, there would be no call for individuality. All art would be similar, there is no demand for what we will be offered next year by way of contemporary arts and crafts. The germs of these ideas are still contained within the minds of those who will originate them and offer them for sale. It will not be until then that we are able to decide individually if we like it, or wish to purchase it. This also applies to you. The key to all this is that for whatever you make there is a buyer. They may see it on the day it is finished and it will fly out, or they may not see it for a year. The more people that see your work the more readily it will sell.

You may be, or be considering becoming, a maker simply because that is what you want to do. To enjoy making things and working for yourself. You should, of course, be aware of pitfalls as well as the joys awaiting you, and have considered them carefully, although sometimes, perhaps, we can be too over-cautious. 'This life is not a dress rehearsal' has become an overworked cliché, but none the less true. We must not waste the opportunity and die wishing we had at least had a go. Quality of life has to come into this equation, and if you are able to travel through life doing what you want ninety percent of the time, this has to weigh heavily against large salaries for a job you would not be happy with. The price you must pay for this is to learn skills that may be abhorrent to you, such as marketing, and be prepared to spend the ten percent of your time working hard at ensuring the other ninety percent is as you would wish.

These are the main motivating forces behind most designer/craftsmen and makers. All are possible to a greater or lesser extent, if, when the going gets tough you go back to what motivated you in the first place and say to yourself 'Am I achieving what I set out to do?' Hard work and skills you did not know you would require will play a very important part. There will be times when it appears that you will need these abilities rather than your ability to create and that is when you must rationalise what you are doing, reassure yourself that you are getting where you want to go and that you are still enjoying the journey.

Knowing what is driving you and what you are aiming for can be very useful, most of us have a aim in life and careful use of long and short term goals will help us achieve it. Mine was to complete this book. As you can see, I have achieved that one, and now I am working on something new. Yours may be an exhibition you would like to organise with fellow craftworkers and artists, to find the time to promote your work more effectively, to still be a craftsman or artist by the end of the year, to take on a partner or to follow up any of the seemingly good ideas that float in and out of your mind from time to time. Without a plan these things can drift; in years to come you will look back and wonder why they did not happen – I was going to do this, but nothing came of it.

To stop this avalanche of possible wasted opportunities you must first define your goal and write it in bold letters at the top of an empty piece of paper, leaving plenty of room to fill on the rest of the page with steps of smaller targets along the way.

It would be impossible to effectively present any particular goal or set of circumstances for illustration here, so I will lay only a broad outline to give you an idea of what I am getting at.

You feel that there is a large market to be tapped in your area and that some local publicity would help you to reach those people and thereby increase awareness of your existence and eventually your sales and your client list. Your goal therefore, is to get your work promoted in the local press, quality magazines and on local television and radio. Write this boldly at the top of your paper with a date when ideally you would like to have completed the project. Whilst this is your goal, your initial step is to do the research work involved, selecting the papers, magazines, television and radio programmes. Write this initial step at the bottom of your page with the date that you intend to start. It would perhaps be feasible to have completed this work within a month, therefore note down the date when you would wish this part of the project to be finished and move on to the next step. In this instance it will be to establish the names of the contacts within your chosen newspapers, etc. and make an index of them. Give yourself another date when this is to be completed by and so on to the top of the page, adjusting dates and the definition of each step as you go ensuring that you are realistic in your expectations of what you will be able to achieve within certain periods of time. It can be disheartening not to reach one of the steps on time, but so satisfying to cross them off early. You will now have a series of steps towards your set goal. Some of the steps will obviously be more difficult to define and to tie down with dates. In the example given above the indefinable part will be the subject content of the press release and this snould be a constant unknown factor, noted beside every step until you have decided upon the subject and it has become a known factor. The writing of the press release then becomes one of the steps, to be put in place and bounded by deadlines.

This is your master plan and you will find that if you place it beside your bed or in your office – somewhere where you will read it every day – your mind will become more receptive to opportunities, ideas will spring more readily from the subconscious as to how to achieve these steps and goals. Keep a note book with you, you will be surprised how often ideas and solutions connected with this project will manifest themselves as you work, sleep and play. You will need to be able to record them immediately, there is nothing so elusive as the good idea you wake up with. It is such a good idea that you feel that you cannot possibly forget it, but sure enough, later in the day, when you are trying to recall the idea to tell a colleague, the chances are it is gone.

Much is made these days of our brain having two levels, of it being a very sophisticated computer if only we knew how to programme it to realise its potential. Reading this plan through daily is the equivalent of programming your mind which will work away subconsciously night and day. Whilst you may or may not go along with this idea, I have to assure you that it is possible to set your brain tasks and allow it to come up with ideas and solutions. This is not going to be one of those 'Sincere, Self-improvement' paragraphs, you will find references to whole books-full in the bibliography. Suffice to say that I have experience of it, and in fact for some things have come to rely on it. Try it for yourself with your list of goals.

Read your list through daily as I have suggested, and also read peripheral material to do with the project in books, newspapers, magazines, etc; this is best done in the evenings before bed. As you carry on with your daily routine the subconscious part of your brain will work on your project. The more information that you take in the more material it has to work with. It is not necessary for you to sit like Rodin's *Thinker*, but relax and go about your normal activities and be ready with the pen and paper when the ideas pop to the top. Jot down all your ideas – evaluate them – perhaps incorporate them into the master plan.

I have even found that this works with significantly important problems. My husband and I have gone to bed going over every option of a difficulty to arrive sometime during the next day both with the same solution. When this solution has been given the closest examination it has always appeared to be the right one. Fairies at the bottom of the garden? – you may be right. But if it works – don't knock it.

Your goal does not need to be earth-shattering, it could be to spend some time on promotional work, whilst still fulfilling all your working commitments and keeping your cash flow stable. Or it could be as ambitious as a promotional tour of a foreign country. The method is the same, start at the beginning, and fill in the smaller targets. Think of it as a train journey, and each smaller item a station on the way to the final destination. A great Chinese proverb, we are told, is that a journey of 1,000 miles begins with but a single step.

This system can be applied to all aspects of your work. Stretch your horizon and aim for the top, the size of your dreams will be the only limiting factor. It is not possible in one gigantic leap. Build your ladder and make your first step, and in years to come you will be able to look back without regrets. You will either have achieved your goals, or you will know that the attempt was made, but that particular goal was unattainable and the reasons why.

Reading through your goals regularly will also serve to ensure that, should an opportunity arise that you wish to pursue, the decision that you make at this juncture is a firm, conscious decision and not a drift, because it seems to be the best thing on offer. Do not be afraid, if a super opportunity does come along, to put your goals on hold. There is no defeat in postponement, or even abandonment if the whole concept seems, upon analysis, to be unworkable.

You read stories all the time of great achievements by people from all walks of life, sometimes against seemingly impossible odds. It follows, therefore, that it is possible for you to achieve your goals, it will only be your own concept of your abilities and the limitations of your expectations that will hinder you. Write down your first goal, list your stepping stones and you will soon find that you begin to achieve the smaller goals, take them one at a time and move forwards at every opportunity. The success of your first attained goal will spur you on to a more ambitious one next time.

Success, the ultimate goal, can be measured in different ways. Only you will know if what you have achieved is that which you set out to achieve and are therefore successful in that particular aspect. It may be helpful to define for yourself what you are seeking by way of success, so that you know what you are aiming for and are able to recognise it when you get there. Other peoples' gauges of success are not necessarily relevant. For example, the perceived notions of the so-called 'yuppies' during the boom years of the early 80's when you were only considered successful if you drove a new car, wore the latest fashionable suit, and carried a mobile telephone and a personal organiser. Shallow symbols of status are not necessarily any indication at all of a successful person.

You must be able to recognise varying degrees of success in yourself and your own work, and stop, even if only for a few moments, and enjoy the feeling. The successful completion of your first commission, first year as a craftsman, first exhibition, five years as a craftsman, etc. etc. – enjoy each milestone.

CHAPTER THREE

You

Throughout the course of a normal year you will probably meet with your current and prospective clients, other agents who may sell your work, the press, bureaucrats, fellow craftsmen, organisers, suppliers, etc. and it is these people that will assist in the building of your reputation. Not only will your work speak volumes, but so will the way you interact with these people. Apart from normal courtesy and good manners you must learn to be reliable, to project a quiet, positive, self-assured manner and how to treat your customers to give yourself the best chance of making a sale or receiving a commission.

It is absolutely essential to be reliable throughout your business particularly when dealing with your clients. If you make and sell something that people can collect or add to it would take an act of faith on the part of the client to buy the first piece of a set and commission the balance from a craftsman who made appointments that he could not keep, made unrealistic deadlines and varied his prices and the quality of his work. Such actions would not instil the customer with the confidence that the maker knew what he was doing, would be able, willing or committed to finishing the commission to a set standard and agreed price, or in fact that he would be in business for any length of time.

This may appear to be basic common sense, nevertheless I have met such craftsmen. It can only serve you well to put yourself in the place of the client. He comes to you, a jeweller say, for a gift for his partner at Christmas. He needs to know that it will be up to the standard of the pieces he has seen that first attracted him to your work. He needs to know that it will be ready for Christmas. He needs to know that if he has purchased correctly and his partner likes the piece then he can commission more from you. And just as important, he needs to enjoy the whole process. The obverse of this situation is too frustrating to contemplate.

You may have become a craftsman because you want to lead a slower, more relaxed lifestyle and the previous paragraph may sound as if you are rejoining the rat race. This does not have to be true. Give honest dates to your clients. If the work cannot be made by Christmas is it better to say so, and perhaps suggest that he gives his partner copies of the preparatory sketches for

Christmas so that she too may enjoy a visit to your workshop whilst the work is in preparation, and collect the piece in January, than to have the client cancel the order on Christmas Eve in a frustrated rage. He can rightfully demand his deposit to be returned and you can be sure you will have lost the customer for good. Others will hear of his unfortunate commission, and a lot of harm will be done to your reputation. He may well not be prepared to wait until January, but he will respect your honesty and he may come back.

Likewise with your dealings with galleries and other sales outlets – be reliable. If you have agreed to six pieces for an exhibition, the subject of each piece, its composition, its price and the delivery date, be sure that that is what you deliver. Catalogues have to be printed, perhaps a photograph is to be featured and space allocated. The gallery director will have been advising clients of the pieces to be exhibited. You will do yourself no favours to take five pieces instead of six or to change the subject, composition or price. At the time of the exhibition it is your reputation that is harmed as the staff have to explain why something featured in the catalogue is not present. If the alteration is small, perhaps the relationship with the gallery and the clients will not be harmed, but if it is large it will be remembered and it is not difficult to imagine the scenario: 'Thomas brought a set of six napkins instead of a 10ft wall hanging for the last exhibition, we will only use him again if we have to!'

It is easy, as you become more established and get to know some of your clients better, to say to yourself 'This piece is for Mrs Smith, she will not mind if it is a bit late'. Do not do it. Mrs Smith came to you, and has stayed with you because of your work, your reputation and the enjoyment of buying from you. Do not begin to chip away at the relationship and your reputation. She will cease to enjoy the experience because you have, by your lack of reliability, introduced an element of exasperation. You will probably, therefore, eventually lose her custom and you have lowered your standards and initially, perhaps, got away with it. This is the slippery slope; where will it end?

It takes a longer time to make a reputation than it does to destroy it, and reliability is an essential part of that concept. From seemingly trivial matters, such as punctuality for keeping appointments, returning telephone calls and sending out quotations through to deliveries and taking part in important events, seek to ensure that reliability becomes second nature.

To acquire and maintain a positive attitude would appear to be a nebulous concept, but no less an important consideration than some of the other peripheral subjects tackled within the scope of this book. It can affect the way you respond to situations, the way you start your day, treat your clients, cope with criticism and rejection, the impressions you make on people, your ability to cope with difficulties and successes.

Sales are of course a major boost to a positive attitude about your work. Your client is telling you that not only is he prepared to pay the price to own this piece, but also that he likes it so much that he want to place it in his home and look at it every day. A very definite boost to the moral and the bank balance. But important customers cannot and do not appear every day of the week.

It is sometimes necessary, therefore, to employ methods to encourage in ourselves a positive attitude so necessary to banish our own negative thoughts let alone the negative responses of others. We do everything we can to 'stack the cards in our favour'. There is no other phrase that sums up so well exactly what I am advocating all the way through this book. At every opportunity we must seek even the tiniest of opportunities that can be used to our advantage. In your work, presentation, press, public relations, research; all the time every aspect is as well done as it can be, and next time it is even better. Your plans and ideas are carefully laid out, analysed and constantly updated. You keep on top of your finances and time management, nothing is left to chance so that with a quiet confidence you become very positive about yourself, your work, and your ability to successfully market it and run your business.

Most things can be done, it is the 'How' that is the difficult part of the equation. Seemingly insurmountable problems are best tackled in a positive way by considering that 'It can be done – but how?', rather than the negative response of 'No – It cannot be done.' Sometimes it helps to start at the end of a difficulty or project rather than the beginning and decide HOW it can be achieved, as with goal setting. Not only is this method ideal for goals as laid out in Chapter 2, but it can also be very useful for pressing difficulties, such as the payment of a large account, eliminating one's overdraft, etc. Start at the end: I must repay my overdraft, HOW can I do it? List the alternative ways, tackle the project from different and more positive aspects, make it into a goal, and take steps towards it.

All of these small but definite steps you take to ensure that you feel positive and confident about yourself and your work help you to deal with the negative responses of others. It is no good pretending that these have no effect, that the people with the buckets of cold water do not know what they are talking about, that they are uneducated, that they know nothing about art, craft, craftsmanship or how to market it.

In my own experience I have encountered time and again the doubters who would have you believe that it is not possible to succeed with your chosen occupation, that you could not succeed in selling the work at all, let alone create a demand for it. I have been able to prove them mistaken. You must always be positive about your abilities to create and market, and strive to do your best at every opportunity.

I am not saying that it is always easy to be positive, but I have given you the tools to fight the negative. When you are turned down by a gallery or an exhibition organiser it is important that you ask why. Some will not tell you, but if you know that your work is as it should be, that your presentation is smart and that you have done your homework thoroughly with regard to the suitability of your work for this venue or event, then you will know that when you are turned down there will be a very good reason for it. But not necessarily the one that comes to lodge itself in your mind – that you are not good enough (if that were true, you should not have approached the organisers in the first place). Taste is subjective – the organiser may not like your work. The prime subject of the display may have been chosen and your work may not complement it. You may be in direct competition with one of the chosen exhibitors who happens to be a close colleague of the organiser. There could be a dozen reasons for your rejection. Do not dwell on the destructive. There are more organisers, more events, and more galleries.

When a commission falls through, again it could be for several different reasons. Humans, being the perverse creatures they are, will decide that they are not good enough, even though the client has explained that his financial circumstances have changed and his liquidation notice has appeared in the paper. Try to accept that it is not always your fault, there can be so many influencing factors in other people's decisions when they are spending a lot of money. They do not need, nor are they always going to explain to you, what those influences are.

Do not allow your work to be placed in negative situations. For example, if a local charity is holding a sale of craft work for a very deserving cause close to your heart and asks you to put some of your work on display. You may feel that you should support them and I would agree with that, but not by showing your work amongst all the other more trivial craftwork that will be on display. It would be more beneficial to you and the charity if you gave your time or real money. The organisers, after all, are not professionals at organising or running exhibitions, it is not their field. It is unlikely that you will sell anything; it is very likely that your work will be badly displayed and trivialised. This is a negative situation and no good will come of it, not to you, your self-esteem, the organisers, or the charity.

It is also easy to become disillusioned with your abilities when you take things at face value. How many times have you seen work on display with huge price tickets? If the maker is well known or the piece a superb example of the art, that is the way it should be. But sometimes the work is inferior to yours, the craftsman or artist unknown to you. 'What's it all about?' you ask yourself. 'Where am I going wrong?' You have allowed a negative response to a totally uninformed situation. All you know is that this piece is 'OFFERED' for sale at this price. Even if it bears a sold label, you do not know whether or not it is a ploy to encourage further sales. I have seen this done on many occasions. You do not know for how long this piece has been offered for sale. If this work is the sole occupation of the maker, he may also be otherwise employed in another occupation or profession, and whether or not the work sells is purely incidental. I have listened to many craftsmen during the course of my consultation work, who erroneously feel negatively about their own progress measured against what they perceive as the progress of their fellow makers. 'But they get such high prices for their work – I could not possibly hope to get that for mine'. I have heard it so many times. What you are seeing is work offered for high prices. You have no concept, though, of how much of the work sells, how often it is produced, how much commission is paid, etc. etc. It is not possible for you to see the whole picture and you should not let uninformed comment undermine your own confidence.

Confidence can assist you in so many ways: when you are writing a press release about your work, when you are mixing with your guests at a private view, being interviewed by the media. Don't allow spurious negative elements to erode it. Learn to recognise information and situations that challenge you and put you on your metal, and those that should be discounted as having no provenance.

Making a sale is not like making a cup of tea, there are no set rules to follow only positive guidelines that you will learn by implementation and experience. When someone is looking at your work it is courteous to greet them and ask if there is any help you can offer. Would they like a brochure, price-list, publicity leaflet, etc. After this exchange of pleasantries they may wish to be left alone, in which case this is what you must do. Busy yourself with work, an inconsequential task or, if at an exhibition, by greeting another client. It is also a good idea to return to the client and ask if they are enjoying the exhibition or display. Most customers will use one of these opportunities or approach you of their own volition to discuss the work, a purchase or a commission. It is then up to you to be positive and enthusiastic about your work, quietly confident and self-assured in your manner and attentive to what the client is saying. Explain how the piece is made, where the materials come from, where you work, what is special about this particular piece. Everything you do leads up to moments such as this. You have 'stacked all your cards', all aspects of the work and the display are special, this client is confirming that, and for him this transaction, too, must be special. Be sensitive to your clients' signals. A couple may wish to confer together, and you should back away and allow them their privacy. Answer their questions honestly and be prepared to be as helpful as is possible – for example, if not allowing the piece to be taken away on approval, offering to take it to their home to see if it is appropriate.

There are those who would advocate the art of salesmanship, and if you feel this may be suitable for your type of work then a course may prove to be very useful, but it should be remembered that modern methods of salesmanship are designed for and taught to the staff of chain stores, insurance companies, car showrooms, etc. You are not selling the run-of-the-mill mass produced item, but something special. Your tools are excellence, confidence, enthusiasm, that you make something special – unique in some cases, the way the piece is displayed, the whole ambience. A special mix for your clients to enjoy, savour and wish to repeat.

When a sale is made, be pleased, reinforce their choice with your own enthusiasm for that particular piece. Be sure you explain how the piece should be cared for, what you offer in the way of after sales service, whether or not the piece is to be delivered and any other pertinent points that have not been covered in your discussions.

Whilst there are no rules to follow to encourage a successful sale, there are very definite rules of what not to do. Never, ever, refer to your clients as punters, neither within their hearing nor without. Colloquially, a punter is considered to be a mug or a sucker, not only is this derogatory and ill-mannered, but it is symptomatic of a bad attitude and ultimately that attitude will convey itself to your clients. In addition, the fact that such things have a way of getting back to people may mean that not only will you lose customers, but also your reputation will tarnish. Do not push a client either subtly or overtly: 'I only have one of these', 'The price goes up on Monday', 'I'll reduce the price'. All these ploys are obvious signals that you are desperately trying to make a sale and can be an immediate turn off. Try to ensure that selling opportunity times are not interrupted, that the telephone answering machine is switched on or that you will not have your attention diverted by children. You know how you like to be treated when shopping; step into the other man's shoes and act accordingly.

As you develop as a craftsman, so will all the peripheral and personal skills important to your business. Only by experience and practice will you be able to gauge the moods and signals of your clients. I can only give you guide lines and they will need different application and interpretation for different clients and situations. The most important rule which will never change is that everything – the work, the display, and the way you treat your clients, must be special.

CHAPTER FOUR

Your work

Your work is the most important part of your business and you must learn to be constructively critical of it or you must find someone whose opinion you value and listen to them. I don't mean your wife, mother, husband or the next door neighbour, people who wouldn't dream of upsetting you and think everything that you do must be wonderful. The biggest problem with an analysis of your work is that those who are knowledgeable and know what they are talking about are understandably reluctant to be critical of another's work. Failing this, stand back and try to see what you are offering through the eyes of an informed critic. Imagine you are that critic determined to find fault with that which is displayed before you.

There are now many courses, seminars and summer schools held or run by good dependable designer/craftsmen. Provided you do your research as to which course you should attend, ie. whether or not it will fulfil your requirements, it may well be a good idea to participate in one of them. You will be keeping yourself up to date, making yourself aware of what is going on in your field and confirming that there is always room for improvement. Obviously, it is better if you are well qualified to determine for yourself whether or not your work is of a high standard, but keeping your eyes open all the time and being constantly willing to learn will help.

Everyone will have a subjective opinion about design, but you will know if the design does not work, if it does not sit well on the eye (unless of course that was your intention), if next time you would not 'see' some particular aspect in a different way. It is not an area that should be neglected, as it can be by so many craftsmen.

Furniture makers will lovingly choose a particular timber for its grain, spend long hours hand working the piece for the satisfaction that that will give him, the dovetails fitting perfectly, the best finish that can be produced, but neglect the elements of the design. Then they will wonder why no one examines the piece closely to see the excellence of his work. It is the initial impact that brings the customer nearer for a closer examination. If you have not caught their attention with the first impression all your hard work has been wasted.

Will the bracelet snag on clothes? Are the chairs comfortable to sit on? The mugs a pleasure to drink from? Does the piece perform its allotted task, whether that be decorative or functional?

Is your work as reliable as the equivalent mass produced product? Are the seams sound? The colours fast? The functional ceramic vessels watertight? etc. etc. The factory-made items will be guaranteed in these respects, the simplest and cheapest items will fulfil their role adequately and will be readily replaced if they are faulty. Your work, therefore, must be at least as reliable, if not more so. If you are selling away from home, this question could be a stumbling block for the client, and a source of irritation if the goods are found to be faulty and need to be returned.

You will also know if the workmanship is not as it should be: perhaps the technical expertise could have been better, or the finish improved upon.

How have you identified your work? Many craftsmen sign and identify their work in different ways and you must choose the one that suits your work best. Do not apply sticky labels to it; not only does it look like a cheap afterthought, but with time it will attract dirt and become illegible. The glue will break down into a revolting sticky mess. If the label was not removed at the time of purchase it will be removed at this stage and will be unable to continue to proclaim that it was you who had so little regard for your work that you stuck a cheap label on it. Do the job properly, having due regard to the piece, how you want to sign it and the job you are expecting this identifying mark to do for you.

Look at other work, go to exhibitions of good work, go to museums. Don't live and work in isolation. Books are free from the library; read and study. If jewellery is your forte, as opposed to ceramics or textiles, your research is only different, no less important. It all sounds terribly boring, but you can lighten the burden by sharing it. Take your partner or friend with you on your expeditions, find a good pub or tea shop for refreshments and discussion, make an outing of it. Keep a diary or a sketch pad and grow in knowledge and ideas. I'm not advocating the copying of another's design, (it is in fact worthy of mention that the copyright laws are now very tight and you should be familiar with the way they affect your work) but training oneself to benefit from the good and bad workmanship and design available for you to see and study. How the work is displayed will also have an influence on how you see it; observe how the surroundings prejudice your feelings of the work.

It is no good trying to sell an inferior product. Look at your work. Is it just good or is it special? Is it worthy of you? With every piece of work you do you must stretch yourself, no matter how mundane the piece you are working on – this toilet roll holder is going to be the best ever toilet roll holder. With this philosophy, no matter how good a craftsman you already are, your work can only improve. Never believe you have arrived, no matter what the press may write of you, there will always be new knowledge to gain and improvements to make.

Don't compromise. It is far better to make a well designed, well made bread and butter item to keep money ticking over, and work uncompromisingly on your special pieces than to allow yourself to be pushed into corners by customers and circumstances which appear to demand a lowering of standards and cheaper prices.

There is a saying 'The poor are always with us', the obverse is also true – The rich are also always with us and are generally more discerning. They know quality when they see it, and are used to paying for it. The only fault anyone should ever be able to find with your work is that they themselves cannot afford it. Someone else can and will.

Never stint on quality. Well conceived ideas badly executed, because they would take too long to make well, can result is no sales at all. It can be difficult when working on a piece as the hours tick by to feel that you will be unable to sell the piece for more than you had initially envisaged to allow for the extra time that it is taking. The pressure to reduce quality or to hurry a speculative piece is usually as a result of concern about cash flow, ie. your need to sell the piece as soon as it is finished. However, unless you have a stack of unsold work that is never likely to sell you must have confidence in the fact that everything you make will sell eventually. If the piece is well designed, well made and marketed, yes it will; on the other hand if it is well designed and made, but finished in a rush to keep under your hypothetical ceiling then no, it may not. Surely it is better that the cost go up by a relatively small amount from your self-imposed ceiling so that the potential customer cannot fault the piece and is therefore willing to go the extra mile as it were, than for him to feel that the piece has not been finished to the same standard as the rest of the workmanship and therefore does not purchase the piece? It makes sense to do the job properly in the first place. If you have serious misgivings about your imagined ceiling or if the piece is a commission that you have underestimated then pride must take over and the job finished properly in your own time. You will not be the first and you certainly will not be the last person to finish something in their own time from pride. There is no shame in this kind of pride. You will ensure that your customer is happy and much more likely to return – look upon it as an investment.

You may feel that your work is already special, but have you considered every detail? A retailer of top quality antique clocks and musical boxes decided there must be more he could do to ensure his pieces were extra special. Everything was beautifully restored and polished, excellence was his byword and one would think that there was no room for improvement. The items were presented in appropriate surroundings, they looked perfect, they sounded absolutely right, they were polished to a tactile perfection. What more could he do? Following a suggestion from a craftsman, he polished the insides of the boxes and clock cases with a pure turpentine-based beeswax polish, a smell reminiscent of the workshop of an old traditional craftsman. Now they smelt right as well. Another card stacked in his favour, another pleasurable experience for the client. Analyse your work in this way and see what improvements you can make.

You must remember that whatever your retail outlets, be they your own home or workshop, galleries, fairs, exhibitions or shops, it is you who shows your work to the customer, gallery owner, or whoever may in the end be representing you and promoting your work and you must have the confidence to sell yourself well to them and convince them that your work is worthy of their attention. How can you do this if you know the piece you are all looking at is not the best that you are able to produce? It is difficult enough to put your work on the line for other people to accept or reject, but if you know that the piece could have been better for a few hours' extra work then you are mentally stacking the cards against yourself.

If your work is of a poor quality and if you've got the nerve to offer it for sale, some tatty craft shop will take it and the general public will see it, turn it over in their hands or run their fingers across it, and wonder who the devil you think they must be to offer them such junk. Whether you realise it or not you are doing grave harm, not only to yourself and your reputation as a craftsman, but to the craft market place generally.

Always push yourself that little bit further in design and workmanship. Don't let yourself, your clients or other craftsmen down. You are on a journey and even a snail goes forward; don't be a crab or a stone or you might just as well go out and get a well paid job with less hours.

CHAPTER FIVE

Presentation

The way you present yourself and your work is another important aspect of the whole promotion and marketing package. From one end of your operation to the other, your work, your business and you yourself must be presented in the best possible light. People like to buy special things, you are making special things and therefore the whole experience for the buyer must be special. The work, the paperwork, literature, photography, packaging, selling space, delivery, after sales service and yourself.

You can do little to change yourself, nor should you, but you can ensure that your manner is always positive and polite and that you do not denigrate the work and achievements of your contemporaries. Some makers have the mistaken belief that they are the best in their field and are not afraid to make that claim. Bad manners and a lack of modesty will endear you to nobody. Due regard should be given to the appropriate attire for different occasions. To stay in one's dirty working clothes to make a delivery to a client shows a scant disregard for them, their home or how important the transaction is. You do not have to dress in your best suit, especially if you have some assembly work to do, but you should be prepared to sit and chat a while over a drink if invited. One of the most difficult tasks is to stay alert and cheerful at exhibitions and craft fairs, but it is so important. Eating on site, chatting to fellow craftsman or reading a book are just a few of many seemingly trivial activities by which some visitors will be put off.

Take a good long look at your selling space and how your work is presented to the public, be it your own or galleries and shops where your work is displayed. There is little you can do to improve a retail outlet over which you have no control. Place your work carefully in the first place and ensure that the standard is maintained. If it is not, then find another venue. Your own selling space is, however, much more manageable and you can seek to improve it at every opportunity. Keep abreast with how other similar work and products are being displayed, always be receptive to new ideas as to how you may improve your own facilities. Maker's display areas can be divided into three main types: your own shop or gallery, a storage area for finished commissions and speculative pieces awaiting placement, and an improvised corner of the work-shop to show pieces to best advantage to visiting clients.

It would be impossible to advise here how each individual maker should display their work. It would merely be my opinion, and I am certainly no interior designer or specialist in display. There would be no room for individuality or flair. These are simple guidelines that can so often be overlooked.

Showrooms should be well laid out and inviting, the decor should not detract from the work but seek to complement it. Most galleries and craft shops use white as a neutral colour with wooden or equally neutral floors. This may not suit your work, but you will find when you come to change the decor of your showroom that a good small interior decorating firm can be very helpful, and may come up with ideas that you had not thought of. This need not be a costly exercise; some of these places sell the paper and paints for you to do the work yourself, but are more than willing to offer suggestions. If you choose an unusual colour of paint, make sure that you have enough to do touch-up work for the duration of this particular scheme.

Think carefully about your wall and floor space with regard to displaying the work to best advantage. Your clients have to be able to see it properly, the access should be clear and uncluttered. Display cases should be purchased or made by a professional. Plinths can be very useful and versatile, even furniture will benefit visually and will be better protected by being an inch or two off the ground. They are a less difficult proposition than display cases and can be made in various shapes and sizes of chipboard, then painted with a matt finish or covered to suit the overall decor. There can be many other materials used in various sizes for plinths: eg. terracotta flowerpots upside down; concrete hollows; large and small dimension plastic and cardboard tubing painted or covered; rough sawn or highly finished blocks of wood; rocks and large pebbles, etc. etc. Whatever you are making think carefully about how you are displaying it. Could it be improved, could it be done more imaginatively? Draped fabric can also be used to good effect, either complementing or contrasting with the overall scheme. Do not forget during this exercise that it is the work that is of prime importance, with the decor you are setting the tone and the ambiance, providing a background. Lighting is an important consideration and must be chosen to suit your specific needs. There are now so many different lighting schemes giving totally different effects that it can only be beneficial to do a little research to discover exactly what is available.

Choose a means to identify and price the work that is clear yet unobtrusive. Avoid hand written sticky labels that are attached to the pieces. Ensure that you have a clear sign giving your opening times, name and address and telephone number.

Having created the ambience, keep the area clean. Put aside a specific time every day for dusting; twice a week or as required to clean the floor; once a week to clean windows, polish where necessary, change and water flowers or plants; once a month to attend to the outside, for example washing the shop front, sweeping the street, removing weeds or whatever. If you have an outside directional sign away from your premises, this must be kept smart, clean and visible.

If your showroom does not have windows directly onto the street and the volume of visitors is low, it may be a reasonable idea to have your lighting system set on a trip switch. This will give a much better impression to your visitor, than you switching on the lights as you enter the showroom. A trip switch can be easily and cheaply fitted, either by yourself if you are competent or by an electrician. Heating in the winter is not as easily catered for, but I would suggest that background heating would be beneficial for the showroom and your work, and it would prevent the place smelling musty and unused. Storage heaters are unobtrusive, relatively cheap to run and may be the answer to the problem. Think around it and do what is best for your own particular circumstances. Huddling around a fan heater you have just switched on will not only create a bad impression but could affect sales. When you are cold it is difficult to think straight. How can you expect your customer to make a serious purchase under such conditions?

Some of these guidelines can be applied to the storage space in which you keep commissions until they are collected. Pieces have not ceased to be important because they are finished and you want them out of the way. Look objectively at this storage area. Does it look like the place where great things should be stored. Whether it is big or small it is equally as important as a showroom, more so if you do not have a showroom on site. Imagine for yourself the impression given to a client visiting on the off-chance that you might have something new to show him, or even, to see his own newly commissioned piece. Here it is, in this cold, dark, dusty room. How much better, if finished commissions, and one or two speculative pieces were stored, or even displayed if space permits, properly. The area may only need a good clear out and a coat of paint, or you may be able to do greater things with it. Your work is special – treat it that way.

It is slightly more difficult to set up a small display area within your own workshop. Space may be at a premium, but you do not wish to be caught off guard should a client call in. Look objectively at your workshop, there must be some way that an impromptu area can be quickly assembled. A roll of wide paper on the wall above the bench with a directional spotlight perhaps. It can be that rudimentary or far more sophisticated if you so wish. How much better the piece will be displayed, against a backdrop with a light on it, than simply placed on the workbench.

It is not beyond the bounds of possibility that your clients will visit your workshop. The exterior should always be clean and tidy and the interior should look as if it is a place where good things are made.

Setting up an exhibition will present many of the problems dealt with in this chapter, and a few more. All the eyesores should be identified during the run up to the exhibition and possible solutions sought. While draped fabric can solve many problems, too much of it can begin to look like a Victorian parlour. Whether or not there are facilities to hang items on the wall should have been ascertained when the venue was being chosen. Most venues have hooks on the wall, but very rarely where you will need them, some may have picture rails with fixings. You will be bound by the colour scheme of the venue, your display equipment should complement or contrast, but not clash. Allow plenty of time for setting up, although you may have worked out a floor plan items may look better in different places. You may be restricted by both existing lighting and where your own supplementary lighting can be placed. Extra lights are generally a must at an exhibition. There are several different ways to tackle the problem, from elegant floor standing spotlights to building a frame for spotlight tracking that you could hang from strategic points. They should not be obtrusive or point at your audience; it is very difficult to look at a piece with a spotlight catching your eye. Choose what will suit your work and your venue. Only you know what effect you are trying to achieve and the ambiance you are trying to create. If you use flowers or plants to enhance the display, they should be chosen and arranged by a professional or very competent amateur flower arranger to ensure that the arrangements help create the desired effect. When you think you have finished, tour your exhibition objectively, make sure all the pieces are shown off to best advantage and are all accessible. That the flowers are well placed and will not damage the pieces either with pollen or sap; flower arrangements must never be placed directly on to exhibits without adequate protection. There should be plenty of room between each exhibit or plinth for your guests to be able to move around comfortably and the emergency exit should be clearly visible.

When you are completely happy with your layout, make sure the floor is clean. dust all the pieces and place identification numbers beside each piece to match the price list. This looks so much better than price tickets or cards. Check your fabric drapes, if you have used any, to ensure no frayed ends are showing. Touch up your plinths if necessary. If you are to use credit card signs display them discreetly with the no smoking sign on the table holding the visitors' book.

After the private view keep the exhibition clean and tidy, constantly check the fabric drapes for raw ends and any signs of disarray, ensure that scuff marks on the plinths are touched up in the evenings and that the flowers are kept watered and fresh.

There will be many other occasions when you will have the opportunity to display your work. The above guidelines should cover most eventualities, but continue all the time to look at what is happening around you and be receptive to new ideas.

Having sold a piece the work does not stop there. How will it get to where it is going? First it must be packaged, not in some old bit of newspaper that you happen to have lying about, but in new appropriate wrapping materials. Self assembly cardboard boxes can be bought from a wholesaler, not only in various sizes, but also in various patterns and colours. Likewise tissue paper, polystyrene beans and other packaging materials. When delivering furniture, an old blanket may indeed be the best possible protection for the piece, but why not bubble pack first, neatly administered, and then a clean, old blanket whilst it travels? On arrival at the destination, remove the blanket and fold it tidily away, allowing delivery of the piece, safe and beautifully wrapped. Never deliver anything on a roof rack, or in some clapped-out old heap; beg, borrow or even hire transport appropriate for the occasion. It is a good idea to check the goods for any damage that may have occurred in transit, half a mile down the road from the customer's house. Should the worst have happened and it cannot be put right on the spot, telephone, make your apologies, go home and fix it. Never deliver damaged goods. Be prepared to spend time with the client arranging the piece in place if necessary. Go cleanly and tidily dressed. Every aspect you project is saying something about you and how you regard your work and your customer. Stack the cards – make positive signals.

If an item is to be posted, depending on your own ability and the fragility of the piece, maybe it would be wise to have it packaged by experts, or if it is a regular occurrence to have the appropriate packaging designed and made. Less fragile items are of course easier. Make the parcel a joy to receive, pack it beautifully with care and pride, type the to and from address labels tidily. Again, we are not forgetting that the contents of the parcel are special, send it, therefore, by a recorded, registered, overnight or even special delivery, depending on the circumstances, and then telephone to ascertain safe delivery.

A proper back-up service is also essential to ensure that your client knows he has bought something special. When the piece is delivered, taken or sent, it should be made absolutely clear to customers that should they need to call on you for any reason connected with this purchase, from polishing and cleaning to breakages, that you will be only too willing to respond. I appreciate that with less expensive pieces this may not be practical, but with bigger pieces it is imperative. This not only removes the concerns they may have for the fragility of a piece, or how it should be cared for but also allows you another opportunity for contact in the future – good sales practice and good P.R. We have enjoyed many a glass of wine and renewed contacts whilst Ian has cleaned and polished a piece of his work. The field of art and craft has so many opportunities for warm, social, interaction and at times this more than compensates for the isolation.

When you send a letter, invitation, set of plans, quotation, etc. always use good quality paper and envelopes, the quality of what you send should be a reflection of the work you produce. Computer labels give the recipient the impression that they are one of many and not really very important; never use them on correspondence to private clients. Your correspondence should stand out amongst their everyday mail as something special.

Again and again we come back to the word special. It is my firm belief that you should strive to make every part of your operation special and I make no apologies for the continued use of the word. From the first tentative enquiry by the client to the delivery or collection, you are making a special piece and the client is having a special experience. In that way you do your best work and not only will they come back, but they will tell their friends. In this way good reputations are built and enhanced.

CHAPTER SIX

Pricing your Work

Money, money, money – everything always comes back to money! Your ability to earn money at your craft gives you the confidence to move forward, to put more into your work knowing that you will get a return for your efforts, to be positive about yourself, your work and your chosen profession – but lack of it can be paralysing.

Initially, you must learn how to price your work effectively for yourself and your clients. It is not possible to arrive new in the market place and expect high recompense for your work, your reputation must be built and confidence established. It is possible, though, to underprice your work, and it is the fine line between too much and not enough that you must establish and move forward from there.

The 'hourly rate': You may feel that you are an artist and above all that. So be it, skip this section, but for the rest of us it is good, sound common sense and it enables you, if the piece is exceptional, to raise the price and make a good healthy profit, or if the work has not gone so well, to calculate a reasonable loss and ensure that at the end of the day you can pay the bills. It gives a good, firm starting point.

So, let us begin with the basics: sit down with a large piece of paper and work out your annual cost of living, ie. mortgage (rent), electricity, gas, insurance, health insurance (compulsory or private), loans for equipment, transport, telephone, your desired earnings (the cost of running your home) etc. I am sure that you are well able to complete your own list. Place a stiff drink close at hand, then add it all up. On revival, divide this telephone number by fifty or forty-eight or however many weeks per year you intend to work. You will note that, although at times you may wish for more, the number of days in a week remains at seven and weeks in a year at fifty-two. You will also note that your desired earnings and number of weeks' holiday become more flexible as you look at the figures.

Now we have the realistic weekly wage/salary, foregoing the impulse to run the car on water or walk everywhere, reduce your family's intake to bread and water, switch off lights and disconnect the telephone. After the initial shock has worn off and you have squared your shoulders to the challenge, you can work out the hourly rate.

You must accept the fact that your day will consist of more than eight hours in order for you to actually do eight hours' work. Some people try to pass on the cost of all the paperwork and running about; others accept it as the cost of working for oneself, doing what you want to do, and if you lose an evening a week on administration, so be it. You must decide for yourself, you can always amend things later, after all, you are not writing this in concrete.

Having worked out an hourly rate and accepted that it will probably take ten hours to do eight hours of practical work you have become a realist. Now comes the difficult part – earning it! Having the courage or otherwise to put the price on your work.

Let me take a figure from the air and use it as an example: let us say £500 a week, £100 per day, £12.50 per hour. Now let us assume it has taken you two weeks to make a piece (it must be fully understood here that I am referring to good quality workmanship and design), according to the set fee the asking price for the piece will be £1000 plus materials and tax if applicable. You may feel that the piece has gone really well and that £1500 would be an agreeable price for it. If you find the right venue and are prepared to wait a little while, give it a whirl, you will never know if you do not try. On the other hand the piece may have gone particularly badly, and perhaps you will have stopped halfway through or continued in the hope of salvaging something. If you are unhappy with the piece and there are obvious flaws, then you must consider whether or not you are harming your reputation by offering it for sale. If, however, you are reasonable pleased with the piece, and feel maybe that it has just taken over-long to produce, you must assess whether or not it will bear the calculated hourly asking price, or should that figure be re-assessed allowing for having had a bad week.

The less mediocre work you show, the more you will find customers accepting the asking price and the less idiosyncrasies there will be in your pricing structure. We all have bad days, and I must agree they are better spent away from the workshop/studio. That does not mean that they cannot be working days. There are a thousand and one other jobs to do, so stay away from the piece you are working on. Tomorrow will be a better day to make up for it. Clients are buying your best work, not a Monday morning job.

One of the big drawbacks with the hourly rate is the imaginary ceiling that you feel that the customer will pay. When you begin to tell yourself that you have been working on this for eight days already, it has therefore cost £800 plus materials and therefore it must be finished today because nobody is going to pay more than that for it. This may encourage you to rush the work and not finish it properly. As difficult as it is you must switch off your mental clock when you work, do the very best you can and finish the job properly. Then ask 'How long have I been doing this?' and make an assessment of the cost. It is easier to sell our imaginary piece for £1000 properly executed and finished than for £800 not finished as well as it should be.

This, you may feel, does not allow for aesthetic considerations, but you need a base to work from to ensure that you maintain your standard of living and can pay your bills. Because a piece owes you two weeks' work it gives you a minimum to start from and you can work up and sometimes down from there. The ups usually more than compensate for the downs, particularly as you become more efficient and used to your pricing structure and the market.

One of the biggest hurdles that most craftsmen/artists have to overcome is the desire to price their work as if they were selling it to themselves or their peers. You can hear them at exhibitions 'I would not pay x for that.' You are not selling to yourselves or your friends and relations with the same earning capacity as you have. You will have to remove your blinkers and see that there are amongst the general populace a percentage of people who have more earning capacity than you do, some of them with more disposable income per week than you will earn in a year. They like quality and they can afford it. On the other hand they do not like to be ripped off and so there is no point overpricing your work. You have to accept that you are providing a service to the public in return for financial reward and regardless of how successful you become you must not lose sight of this. Of course you can expect your wages and profit to rise commensurate with your reputation. It is accepted that the best will always command more than the mediocre. Quality work shown in the appropriate place to the right people will sell for the correct price.

The pricing of commissions seems to be an area beset with concerns – Will they like my ideas – Will they commission the piece – How will I get the price right – If I quote x, what about an allowance for contingencies say x + y? – Or will they not want to pay x and then I will lose the commission. If you have made reasonable calculations and x is the outcome then that must be the asking price. When you discuss the matter with your client it is possible and acceptable to suggest that the final cost could be x plus or minus y, allowing both for contingencies and very smooth execution. Be confident, he must have seen your work before and the cost of different pieces, you will have discussed possible costs during the initial discussions. What he really needs to know is the bottom line which, allowing for hiccups, will be x + y. But do be sure that if the cost is x or even slightly less that you do not ask for every penny agreed. Be sure that if you ask him for less than he is expecting (because it has cost less and not because you are feeling altruistic) not only will he be pleased with the work, but he will know that you have been honest and fair with him. This will further enhance the pleasure he has obtained in the commissioning process and in owning a piece of your work, and certainly increase the likelihood of a repeat commission.

Confidence plays an enormous role in the selling of your work, and it is one of the reasons why a number of craftsmen/artists opt for a selling agency, be it a gallery, craft shop, etc. It can be a nail-biting experience if your cash flow is a little slow and a client visits your workshop/showroom to see what you have available at the moment. It would be wonderful if he were to buy a piece, particularly if you make more expensive items, thereby easing your immediate cash crisis. Whatever you do, do not offer to reduce the price, this will indicate a lack of confidence, a need, hint that all is not as well as it might be. They want to buy from successful people who are going places, so that in the future their purchases will be seen to have been wise investments. If a client is considering spending several hundred if not several thousand pounds, the odd fifty pounds will make little difference to his ability to own the piece if he so wishes.

This is not to say that if you like to give your long-standing clients a little discount then that is your decision, but it should be a careful part of the final negotiations, not an offer to encourage a sale. Discount can be a funny thing, some established customers eventually expect it, some would be affronted at the very idea. Tread carefully, it becomes easier as you become established to be confident that if the piece does not sell today then it will sell in the future and you will not feel inclined to sell it underpriced to a stranger who demands discount. It is very satisfying when this stage is reached and you are able to do this at your own discretion.

It is also necessary that the price of your work increases as the years pass, not only to cover the cost of living, but because clients like to see that they have made wise choices in the past and that you are successful. To this end I have always increased the selling price of my husband's stock by a percentage every January. You may like to do the increase more scientifically, by re-calculating your costs, that is your choice.

Another thorny issue connected to pricing your work is the selling venue. If your showroom is your sole outlet, then there is no problem; the difficulties arise when your work is out at various retail outlets and apart from capital city venues where everyone expects to pay more there must be a consistency in the selling price of your work. Outlets will want anything from 10–50% commission and it would be better to approach this subject from the selling price down than from the cost price up. That is, if you decide that your work should be offered to the public for £1000 and the gallery require 50%, has your cost price been £500 or less. If your cost price was £550 are you prepared to lose £50 to have your work at this particular outlet? Is it worth £50 or should the selling price nudge up to £1100 to allow for that? How will this affect other venues? Will they be able to sell the work for £1000, or would you prefer to stay with venues whose commission was consistent at about 25–35%. If you do have your work out for sale in this way then you must adopt this selling price at home with visitors to your workshop/showroom. It is not difficult to envisage the unpleasant situations that may arise if you do not maintain an even selling price in the market place. Be sure that if you are undercutting your gallery outlets at home, they will learn of it, and possibly refuse to carry your work. It is a difficult issue; one way around it, of course, is to sell your work to the outlets, they are then free to sell for as much as they wish, but there are very few that will buy.

CHAPTER SEVEN

Commission

Commission, as touched on briefly at the end of the previous chapter, is perhaps one of the biggest bones of contention that artists and craftsmen have. It is the one issue that they all have very strong and almost 100% negative views about. I will try here to look at the issue objectively and offer some valid explanations for its implementation. Why is this the only field where 'sale or return' – 'on commission' applies almost universally?

You will hear the odd artist/craftsmen tell you that the galleries 'buy or they do not get'. This is either bravado or the teller is one of the very few who is in the happy position whereby this is perhaps true of one or two sales outlets where he has proven to be very saleable and has been able to come to this agreement. Or the craftsman/artist's reputation is such that he is at long last able to demand this method of working. Usually the wholesale price will be very competitive. Ninety percent of the time you are being spun a yarn by someone who wishes to impress you – there is a lot of it about in the art and crafts field, it can be very destructive and should be taken with a pinch of salt.

Commission is a difficult concept to come to terms with. I know that it is done now and again in other fields, particularly antiques where one dealer will suggest to another that whilst he does not wish to invest in a particular item belonging to a colleague, he feels it will sell better through his outlet than his colleague's. A deal is struck to move the object to the more advantageous venue and the seller will accept a commission for the more rapid sale of the item at perhaps a more favourable price. This is understandable, as is commission for work sold at exhibitions, but to stock a shop or gallery with unpurchased items, less so.

Is it perhaps because there is no ready consumer market for contemporary art or craft in this country that a hard headed businessman would accept as commercially viable? There are very few art/craft outlets of quality which an entrepreneur would call commercially profitable, even though their stock costs them nothing, payment being made to the maker after the sale of items. Nevertheless, sale or return is the status quo and unless all artists and craftsmen are going to band together today and say 'NO MORE', then it is the way it will continue. So how do we work with it?

We work with it by accepting that the payment of commission on work sold is a payment for a service. All services have to be paid for and you will be able to assess in each case whether or not what is on offer is acceptable for what you are being asked to pay.

Reputable galleries and other retail outlets will have contracts, and terms and conditions for the maker to read and sign. I cannot emphasise enough that these must be read thoroughly. It is in the terms and conditions that sometimes the agreeable sounding commission becomes unacceptable. Not because the amount is changed but because the terms surrounding the payment of the amount becomes unacceptable. For instance, I have recently read an artists' contract with a reputable international gallery; the commission was 50% which seemed reasonable for the prestige and facilities being offered. It also appeared reasonable to take a lesser wholesale price for the work to have it on show at such a venue. What made it onerous was that after the sale, the artist/maker is advised of the transaction, at which time he must then raise an invoice, which will not be paid for three calendar months. Also in the terms the gallery is authorised at the discretion of their staff to make a ten percent reduction in the selling price. Additionally, the insurance was set to allow for only 75% cover of the wholesale price. And so on. The contract was weighted very heavily against the artist/maker.

Some contracts are not this onerous, you must read them carefully and decide what you are getting for your money, and that it is a retail outlet that you can work with efficiently for the benefit of all parties – that is you, the gallery and the client. You are paying for the venue, position, overheads, expertise, prestige; only you can decide whether or not what you are being asked to pay is what you are prepared to pay.

As the price of the work increases it becomes a more difficult issue to resolve. Take a piece of work that involves another maker as well as the original maker, for example a bronze casting or a clock. The maker's price of say £8000 may include say £1000 worth of work already paid to a third party. The gallery working on 50% will mark this up to £16000. The piece sells at £16000 less the discretionary 10% of £1600. The maker will in three months' time get £7200 less £1000 to the third party leaving him with £6200 for his labours and no address of his new client. The gallery on the other hand has made £7200 for the use of their venue, its position, their expertise.

Is it 'unfair, unfair'? Is the piece now established at a new price of £16000? Has it not been prestigious to sell successfully at this venue? Will they not want another piece? Is the fact that you do not have the client's address of such importance, does he not know where to go? On the other hand, had you the

£7200 to spend could you have sold the piece for £16000? Would you have known how to go about it?

Only you can decide, weigh up the fors and againsts as they apply to you and your work. If you already sell reasonably well from your own outlet then it becomes a more difficult and less viable proposition. If a gallery were to approach you with the terms quoted above, then what do you do? If you can sell a piece for perhaps £5000, how do you approach the matter? Of course if the gallery will just take the piece at £5000 and mark it up to £10000 all well and good – maybe it will work and maybe it will not. But if they want their selling price to be consistent with your's, give or take a little, are you prepared to accept £3000 so that they can offer it at £6000? Only you are able to analyse and decide the benefits or otherwise for your own situation.

Commission can take different forms. Recently on a trip to New Zealand, and perhaps the same is true of tourist areas in other countries, I was asked why tour bus drivers should be given 'a hand out'. The maker was affronted that although the tour bus stopped a short way from his workshop and showroom, the tourists were not directed or even encouraged to visit him by the driver and thereby obtain some very acceptable souvenirs. The simple answer to this is 'Why should he?', 'What is in it for him?' It may be a sad indictment of society that very few people now do something for nothing. The tour bus drivers had worked out that it was reasonable to expect commission to deposit forty potential customers on the doorstep and advise them what a good stop this was for authentic, handmade, local souvenirs. It seems equally miserly to me to expect someone to do this service for you and not to reward them – to pay for the service. Step into the other man's shoes now and again, see it from another viewpoint.

Another form, much more subtle, but one that should always be recognised and acknowledged in whatever form seems appropriate, is a 'thank-you' for an introduction. It may simply take the form of a telephone call, a bouquet of flowers, right through to hard cash. If a client introduces a new customer, you obviously would insult him by offering him cash, but not by ringing to thank him and perhaps if it is appropriate a little discount from his next purchase. Family and friends often sing your praises the loudest, and our staff and family have always been rewarded for their time and enthusiasm. Needless to say one's offsprings always prefer cash. It has been my experience to have a new client sent from another gallery, my immediate response was to thank the gallery owner and give her a cheque for ten percent of the selling price. Other craftsmen may refer clients to you, you may work on a quid pro quo basis, he sends them to you and you send them to him. But if it is all one way or isolated incidents then your appreciation of the client's referral should be acknowledged appropriately.

To me, all of this makes good, sound business sense. You may have a little less cash than you would have had, but without all these ambassadors you may not have had the sales. If you took as your right their first referrals with no hint of gratitude even, it is unlikely that they will be so enthusiastic on your behalf again. They will rightly think you ungrateful and not bother next time. It has to be remembered that they have expended time, effort and energy on your behalf, and in the case of the gallery owner, she may well have talked herself out of a sale. It is only courtesy that you thank them and acknowledge their enthusiasm on your behalf in an appropriate way. At most it could cost you ten percent, but ninety percent of a sale is better than a hundred percent of nothing.

CHAPTER EIGHT

Managing Your Money

Having worked out the the basic working principles of your earning capacity, it is then important to keep your finances carefully documented and monitored so that at all times you know your situation.

Keep an updated account of:

Your bank balance.

Who owes you money, how much and when it can reasonably be expected.

Commissions you are working on, when they will be finished and when payment (including interim payments) can be expected.

Accounts payable and their due date.

Accounts you are expecting and when they will become due.

Your stock position, although speculative sales should not be anticipated.

In this way you will be able to properly manage your financial affairs and not lurch from one disaster to the next. You will see if a client needs a reminder, or if you should telephone a creditor and explain that whilst you know the account is due, you will be able to send him a cheque next week. This will put his mind at rest and pre-empt any bad feeling or pressure, but if you have said you will do it – do it.

Money is such a funny thing in that no one seems to like to actually ask for it. It appears to be an embarrassment. It is a commodity like any other and you should not be afraid of asking for it, or to discuss openly methods of payment. It is very unlikely that in the creative field a new client takes work without payment there and then, thereby eliminating one of the major hurdles faced by many businesses. You will be able to decide for yourself when you feel a client has reached trustworthy and established status and can be relied upon to pay for a piece he has taken on approval. When commissions are discussed, so should the fee and method of payment. The timing and amount of initial and interim payments should be set and a method of receiving them settled. If your client is reluctant to pay a deposit, what confidence does this inspire in his willingness to pay interim and final payments?

Whilst you manage all aspects of your business yourself it is possible with a few enforced guide lines to ensure that most of the time you are paid for your work as it progresses, when it is finished, or when it is sold. When other agents are involved, with watertight paperwork you could still wait a long time for a sale from a gallery to filter through, whether or not they are working on sale or return. They may even liquidate while still in possession of your work. This can be taken into account by wording your invoices as follows: 'All goods remain the property of the originator until paid for in full'. This does not, however, allow for them liquidating between selling the piece and paying you.

Even in the best regulated workshops and studios there can still be outstanding accounts that if not handled carefully could become bad debts. It is essential to point out here that a shortage of money can have an adverse effect on peoples' manner and attitudes. You must guard against this if you are the one who is short of money and approaching clients to encourage them to pay; ensure when you contact them that you are in a positive frame of mind and not aggressive. On first contact you do not know why they have not paid, it may be a simple oversight and you do not want to alienate their custom.

How well you know the client, and whether or not they are private or commercial will of course determine your approach. Commercial clients will have their own methods for payment and it should have been established at the outset of the transaction whose terms you were both going to abide by. Unfortunately some large enterprises now consider it good financial management to hang on to money as long as they possibly can. Sometimes this log jam can be broken by a polite telephone call to the initiator of the transaction, or the accounts department, unless there is a problem with the work that you have carried out which should come to light with this telephone call, if it has not been made known to you before. If this initial telephone call fails to work, ie the cheque is not in the post within two days repeat the operation, regularly, every two days if necessary until you are paid. Try to get someone in the accounts department on your side, someone who will actually be able to place the cheque in front of the appropriate official and plead your case. Perhaps you will be able to encourage your contact within the firm who brought you the commission, to intervene on your behalf.

Sometimes a little low cunning may be called for – a colleague of mine was getting desperate. A wealthy Swiss business man owed her a reasonable sum of money, he had always paid promptly and she had had no reason not to send a shipment to him. This time it was different, no amount of reminders or telephone calls produced a cheque. She thought around the problem, and it seemed insurmountable. He was in Switzerland and she in the U.K., he was protected by his secretary at work and a telephone answering machine at home. Then employing a little lateral thinking, she felt that he was very jealous of his public image and would not relish the prospect of his debt becoming common knowledge. She therefore sent an open fax to his head office where it would be seen by his colleagues and staff. The cheque was received by return post.

When it is a private client that has not settled an account, there is usually a reason. If your association has always been amicable and it has been established that the customer is happy with the quality of the work you have undertaken, it is safe to assume that there is a problem and it would be reasonable to ask what it might be. It may simply be an oversight, and you can breath a sigh of relief, but there could be a number of other reasons and the rule of thumb is to stay talking and friendly.

There is no hard and fast way to ensure that debts are settled. If there were, we would not have the many debt collecting agencies that now proliferate in our towns and cities. These I would suggest have a dubious role to play in the pursuit of unpaid accounts, as do solicitors and the small claims court. They are a desperate last resort, and the experience, even if you do get settlement, can be costly not only in money, but in time, energy and personal trauma. Once any of these remedies are set in motion, your client is immediately on the defensive to justify his position. This usually means that he will seek to find fault with an aspect of your work, letters are exchanged which you will brood about, your mind will go over and over the situation, your work will suffer because you are preoccupied, every stage of the proceedings will take an age, trips backward and forward to the solicitor, and at the end a court appearance where your work and reputation will be on the line. No matter who you are or how good your reputation some of the muck will stick. Even if you are exonerated and get settlement bad feelings have been generated and the client will not forget, nor will his friends and acquaintances to whom he will relate the story at every opportunity. A positive result in court is not a certainty, no matter what your solicitor is telling you. The only winners are the solicitors.

What if you lose? How will you cope with that? Not only will you have the bad debt and the ill-feeling between yourself and your client but you will also have the solicitor's and court's fees, the lost time, the hassle, the personal trauma, and defeat. Before you set out on this course of last resort, ask yourself what you have to lose, what you will gain and the cost. Once you have set these wheels in motion it is impossible to go back and talk to your client and possibly settle the matter amicably. Think very carefully before you shut any doors.

Another aspect of money that you should not neglect is keeping good regular accounts. All sales correctly receipted and recorded, all costs carefully monitored and filed. The best method of course is to devote a little time to them regularly depending on the size of your operation. How much easier to sort through your pockets and wallet weekly for the screwed up pieces of paper that were tidy, readable receipts when you were given them, than once a month to spend ages discovering that the particular clothes you were wearing when you visited the hardware shop have now been through the wash. Having a regular regime for this task concentrates the mind and helps to keep it all under control. Whilst you can list your sales and receipts for yourself and carry out the simple analysis required in order to pay your tax quarterly, if you are registered, I would advocate that, regardless of how small your concern, you employ a qualified accountant for the end of year accounts and to deal with the tax man. A good accountant will be worth every penny, not necessarily in hard cash, but the saving in time and sheer frustration. He knows how to draw up and present your accounts; what the tax man needs to know; what is allowable and what is not, etc. etc. You have enough peripheral tasks that you cannot pass on, without trying to undertake this one. Just the changes in taxation resulting from one budget can fill a paperback book of unintelligible jargon. This is a job best left to an expert. Do your research and make sure you find a good one. Do not seek the advice of an amateur, friend or colleague, they may not know or understand recent legislation or rules pertinent to your situation. Uninformed advice for financial matters can lead to difficult problems.

Then there is the question of raising money: to start your business, for a special project, to buy new equipment, to ease cash flow or for one reason or another. This can be achieved in many different ways, through grants, loans, allowances, sponsorships, partnerships or even one's own family.

There are many grants, allowances and sponsorships available, their use is usually very specific and their qualifying requirements quite rigid. It is very difficult for an individual to find out from where they are all available, for what purpose and how to qualify. With the advances in information technology it is becoming easier to discover these things. Not only are there directories published, but there are also firms that specialise in knowing what is available. The best starting point would be your local reference library, and from here you would need to expand all leads until you hit on the one that looks most promising. Reading your trade magazines and literature along with those of closely associated interests will of course help to keep you in touch with what is being offered specifically in your own field. Keeping an eye on the local and national press can also prove fruitful, and whilst they may not publish specific details of a particular grant or allowance, they may be running a story on someone who has just been awarded a grant similar to the one you are seeking. A few well placed telephone calls may produce the contact you are looking for. Always bear in mind that it is impossible for any one body, directory or source to know all of what is on offer and a little research could well pay dividends.

Generally, when you get to the middle of this maze, and have found the grant, award or scholarship most suited to your needs you will also find the instructions on how to apply. Remember first impressions are important, especially when you are not there to represent yourself. To get through the selection procedure your only representative will be the form you have filled in, any accompanying paperwork and photographs. Ensure that everything is done with the utmost care, with pernickety attention to detail. Answer all the questions on the form, first on a blank piece of paper, so that there are no mistakes on the form, and everything fits correctly into the boxes.

Pick your best photographs. If they are to be slides, get out the projector and look at them properly, don't just hold them up to the light and hope for the best. The accompanying paperwork should also reflect the image you are trying to portray of excellence and professionalism. Do not send a C.V. that has been copied so many times it is illegible, or askew on the page. Do it properly, stack the cards. In the event that you are turned down, you will know that it was not your presentation. You will not reproach yourself with 'if only's. Like so many things, you will only get one chance. You will be unable to write back and say 'I am sorry but I left this out, or perhaps this was not clear, please could you reconsider me?'

Banks are a good source of money; there are only four problems: 1) usually collateral is required, 2) there is a charge for the service, 3) interest is charged, 4) the money has to be repaid. No one bank is as good as the next, the branch you use is only as good as the manager that runs it. If you need to work with a bank then the manager of your branch is all important. If you can work within your allowed parameters, not needing to call upon the manager's discretion now and again, then a relationship with the manager may not be that important. Nevertheless, I would advocate the building and maintaining of a good business association, you never know when you may need it.

If you have been with the same bank from an early age, you may already know your manager and have an established track record when you embark on your career in crafts. You may not need to borrow money straight away and feel it unnecessary to advise him of your new occupation, but I would suggest that in the interests of sound business practice you send him a brief letter. Advise him of what you are doing and your plans for the future and possibly enclosing a photograph of your work.

When the time comes that you need to borrow money either for a piece of machinery, the lease on a new workshop, an exhibition, etc. he will have on file what you are doing, how long you've been doing it and any other snippets you have sent him. I'm not suggesting he should be inundated with literature, but kept informed. In this way you have laid the ground for an approach for a loan should you need one.

When you keep your appointment to seek your loan take with you as much information as you can including the past three years' accounts if you have been working as a craftsman for that length of time. If it is a new piece of machinery you require you should be able to supply the cost of the machine, what it will do, how it will improve efficiency and how you intend to pay for it. If the loan is for an exhibition, you should be able to supply the cost of producing the exhibition, (see Chapter 13), what sales you anticipate, and what contingency plans you have lined up against failure. Whatever the loan is for the principle is the same and must be worked through thoroughly.

It can only be to your advantage to supply the maximum of information when seeking a loan. The guidelines set out below are how to work through what will be required should you be seeking a loan to set up a business.

The Product
Furniture Pots Textiles   Good clear photographs

The Market
Supply and demand   Who wants it? – who will buy it? –

Where will it sell?   How much will it sell for?
                                            What competition is there?

Budget
What can be produced   Cost of production
                                            Raw materials
                                            Tools and equipment
                                            Overheads
                                            Wages – even if only yours.

And the inevitable WHY
Why are you doing it?
If you do this well you will not only be giving your manager what he needs to grant the loan, you will also be clarifying in your own mind the how's and why's. You will be setting down for yourself a clear direction and goal; you will be able to see the flaws in your argument, where you need to do more research and tighten up sloppy areas. How much better it would be if you had one or two letters from sales outlets confirming they will take your work, even a few orders or commissions.

Having armed yourself with all the paperwork necessary – not forgetting a copy to leave with him, the other equally important item is yourself. You will be selling yourself as well as your idea, to the establishment. It is therefore important to conform to accepted standards and these may not necessarily be your own. You must be presentable, that is tidily dressed and not shedding workshop debris as you go, with half inch of mud on your shoes from just outside the workshop door. The manager will be looking for confidence, determination and a good clear presentation of your aims and objectives and a sound knowledge of how you will repay the loan.

Not having any collateral, ie. possessions, the title of which can be held by the bank to be liquidated in case of default, will not make the task of obtaining a loan impossible, just more difficult and more expensive. A reasonable rate of interest is between 2–5% over base for a secured loan and 4–7% unsecured.

If the loan is refused, you will generally be told why. Always be prepared to listen and reassess your position. There could be many reasons for refusal and only by listening will you be able to look carefully and objectively at your proposal and either modify it, try other avenues of finance or get a job.

There are further sources of finance, but if you cannot get a grant or an award etc. and the bank won't lend you money you must look seriously at your project and ask yourself if everybody is out of step but you. Can they all be wrong?

If you are still convinced you need the money then there are various alternatives all with a great deal more risk than the bank's. There are loan companies, who will want excessive repayments and probably should be avoided. Your family and friends may be another source, but with great potential for causing rifts. If you do raise the money this way, get the family solicitor to draw up a legal document for repayment, see if you can insure the loan so that if things don't work out the money can be repaid anyway. All in all, borrowing from friends and relatives usually means trouble eventually.

Then there is a partnership – someone who will inject money into your business for a return on investment. Again you must have careful documentation of your transaction drawn up by a solicitor. It may be better to investigate any business expansion or setting up schemes run by the government. Research the matter thoroughly, and ask yourself seriously if you really want a partner? Can the business sustain your wages and the partner's return on investment.

Small local investors are generally a thing of the past. Not all that long ago it was feasible that a well established local solicitor would know of a local business man with funds to invest. This is no longer as common as it was, but there just may be the odd one left about, a possibility you may wish to consider.

Help may come from the most unexpected quarters and not necessarily in the form of money. You may be seeking a source of money to make a move to larger premises more viable. In such circumstances do not overlook the possibility that your local authority, some other body, or even a private individual may have subsidised workshops or studios to let. Always think around your challenges carefully and with an element of lateral thinking. The most obvious answers may may not always be the best.

It would be impossible for me to write a chapter on money without passing on to you one of the most important pieces of advice I have ever been given. It is from an impeccable source, our much admired and respected bank manager for fifteen years, until his resignation. *Always open your mail.* When things begin to go wrong, it is apparently a common tendency to leave the post for another day, fearing the bad news that it may bring. Open it – confront the problems and deal with them. Sometimes it can take a lot of courage to face-up to unpleasant difficulties, but hiding from them will only make them worse.

CHAPTER NINE

Research

Throughout this book you will be admonished to do your research. It cannot be stressed enough that for almost all aspects of your business, research will play an important part. If the findings are properly considered and applied they could stop you from making a serious error and help to improve your judgement.

It is not possible to predict each and every situation needing careful research that you will come across, neither is it possible to know individual circumstances that will alter some of the questions that need to be answered. Within this chapter, I go through common ground for most craftsmen and list some of the necessary questions that it would be helpful, if not imperative, to have the answers to. Some of your research will be specific and it will be simple to discover where to go and in which publications to look to answer your questions. Other aspects of it will be far more nebulous and you will discover answers to questions you did not know you had asked in the most unusual places.

A continually perceptive mind will ensure that you are always travelling towards new and exciting ventures and that you are seeking always to improve your work, the way it is seen, promoted, marketed, and the way in which you conduct your business.

From the college or courses you attend to learn your craft, to the company who supplies your wine for your first private view, nothing should be left to chance. Every avenue should be explored. When you have all the information that you feel it is possible to obtain you are, of course, in a much better position than you were at the outset to make an informed decision.

The problem with research is knowing beforehand what it is you need to know. Each different project should be taken separately and a list prepared.

For colleges and courses you would need to know:

The subject that you wish to study.

Who are the best exponents of this art.

Do they teach at a college, summer school or workshops.

Do you want a full time course or a part time course.

Who else holds courses on this subject and what do they offer.

Do you need a qualification.

Will there be a qualification at the end of the course.

Will these courses cover everything you want to learn.

Will it be possible to supplement one course with another.

How far are you prepared to travel.

What are the costs involved, A) for the course, B) for accommodation.

Are there any scholarships or grants available and would you qualify.

Where to start asking about financial assistance.

As you can see, the more you seek to discover, the more information you will uncover, the better decision you will be able to make. This is the formula that you must apply to each research project.

When you start to work on your own you will need to be able to make judgements about how good your work is, how well designed it is, whether or not it can be better displayed and all this information is available to you if you are able to recognise that you need to ask yourself these questions. All of us must always be prepared to learn and improve and should seek ways to do this at every opportunity. If you find research of this nature dry and dusty you should try to find ways of making it more enjoyable; take a friend with you, reward yourself afterwards, visit a colleague on the way home, etc. You will soon find that as this structured research begins to show in your work and the way you are able to improve your presentation. It will become a more pleasurable activity and one you will look forward to.

Walking the dog in the evenings around the local shopping centre will be seen as an opportunity to observe what new ways of display some of the shops are now employing. What sort of lighting they are using and whether or not the displays work, ie. are they tempting, do they encourage you to go into the shop tomorrow for a closer look. You will have constructive objectives for almost any trip out whether it is an outing to the cinema, past all the fashionable shops or a holiday abroad where you can venture into foreign galleries and shops to see what is happening in your field and how it is displayed.

Books and magazines are also a good source of research within this area of work and display, not necessarily publications limited to your own field. Not all books are available in either the borrowing or the reference library and it may be prudent now and again to actually purchase books that you feel will be useful time and again. Do not blinker yourself; if it is a work and display research period, but you come across some good ideas for exhibition lighting or photographs that convey the feeling you would wish to capture for your work, make notes and store this information along with the rest of that day's findings. This type of research cannot be led by a series of questions to which you are seeking specific answers; it is a continual process of being receptive to good ideas and stimulating environments. Therefore, always be prepared to go somewhere new and be ready to take on board what you see around you. Do not be ready to denigrate and criticise, go with an open mind and weigh up carefully what you see. Your mind is a sponge, fill it with information and learn to reject objectively rather than to dismiss out of hand without considered thought. The better the quality of information and stimuli, the better the resultant influence on your work and its display.

Before you set up a business you will need to research how it is all going to work:

What field of craft will you work in.

What will you make.

Where will you make it.

Do you need planning permission

Have you considered the way your craft will affect your neighbours, and how they may affect you, eg., noise, smells etc.

Will fire regulations apply.

What legal obligations will have to be undertaken, eg. hallmarking.

What equipment will you need.

What suppliers will you use, A) For equipment, B) For raw materials.

What are your start up costs.

What type of insurance will be required.

What are your running costs.

How will it all be paid for.

Where will you sell it.

Which sector of the market will you target.

To target your clientele you must also employ research. You must discover where they live, work, shop and play, and which magazines and newspapers they take. In this way you will know where to place your work in order for them to see it with regard to both the media and promotional and selling opportunities. Once you have identified these areas in your own local town you can gradually spread your net and work on nearby towns and villages.

Always expend a little time researching any selling venues you may consider using:

Is this the right area.

Is this an appropriate venue.

Is the correct calibre of client attracted to this venue.

What else do they sell.

Is your work complementary, a contrast, competition or out of place with the current stock.

Is your work of the same quality, better or worse.

Does the current stock appear to be well looked after.

Are the staff knowledgeable and friendly.

Does the stock appear to turn over frequently.

How long has the outlet been there.

Does it have a good reputation.

Is it financially stable.

Is there a programme of exhibitions.

If you decide to approach an outlet you must then discover:

The name of the person responsible for viewing new work.

The full address of the gallery.

During your initial discussions with the manager you must learn:

The contractual terms and conditions set out between craftsman and retailer.

Any restrictions that may be sought upon your placing work in close proximity to this particular venue.

How they will promote your work.

If you are considering participating in an exhibition, crafts fair or other organised event, many of the previous questions will be valid, but to them you should add:

What have the visitor numbers been in past years.

What are the visitor numbers likely to be this year.

What have been the sales/ commissions generated.

What are the costs involved, A) For exhibiting, B) For travelling and C) For accommodation.

What advance publicity has there been in previous years.

What advance publicity will there be this year.

How will your work be displayed.

Is this event appropriate for your work.

Is there a selection procedure.

It is so easy to be enthusiastic and excited about taking part in a major event and rush headlong into the venture without thinking it through carefully.

Research is not meant to be a big bucket of cold water, more an insurance that if you do decide to take part in something for the prestige, excitement and possible sales, that you do so with your eyes wide open. You will know how much your prestige and excitement will cost you if sales are a little slow. Sometimes it can be a good idea to take part in an event for reasons other than those of pure finance, for example for kudos or experience. All I would advocate is that you consider all angles including the cost, asking yourself if the money is being put to best use – perhaps it is possible to spend less money for more kudos or experience elsewhere.

The research involved in holding your own exhibition can be forbidding, but using this basic list, to which you will need to add or subtract depending on your own specific needs, should be helpful:

Location of venue.

What will be an appropriate venue.

When is the best time to hold an exhibition, A) For your clients, B) For you and C) For the venue

What are your requirements of the venue.

Does the venue cater for most of your requirements.

What further requirements are needed: A) Security, B) Lighting, C) Plinths D) Display material, E) Numbering system, etc.

Will you be able to display everything you wish to exhibit to best advantage, ie. are there places for wall hung displays, or are the walls covered with inappropriate pictures that cannot be moved.

Are the access and parking facilities adequate.

What are the costs involved.

What are the terms and conditions.

When issuing a press release you will also have to embark on a certain amount of research:

Which media channels are likely to be read, heard or watched by your clientele.

Which of these magazines, newspapers, radio or television programmes are appropriate for your item.

To whom should you send your press release.

What are the lead times involved.

As you can see there are always vital questions to be asked, and none more so than when you are seeking a professional to carry out work for you, eg. an accountant, a photographer, an exhibition organiser, an agent, a printer, or another craftsman to whom you subcontract some work or with whom you participate in an shared exhibition.

What is the quality of their work.
Are there references available.
Can you work effectively with these people.
Are they reliable.
What are the costs involved.

You can apply research to joining groups, guilds or associations:

What are the aims and objectives of the Association.
How do they achieve their objectives.
Is it something you would wish to be associated with.
How does it run.
Does it function efficiently and effectively.
What are the advantages of belonging.
What are the disadvantages.
Is it for amateurs or professionals.
Are there restrictions on membership.

In all aspects of your work there will always be another area that will need research: selling your work abroad, expanding your business, exploring the market-place for further opportunities, seeking a new supplier, etc. Try to ask yourself all the questions that you feel you will need answered to help you make constructive judgements and decisions. Do not be afraid to ask people with experience, but be sure to listen to what they have to say. You may not like the reply, but it will be valid and should be added to the rest of your research for analysis and consideration.

Other sources of information will be reference libraries. I have always found the staff in my local branch an absolute mine of information. They always know where to look for the information you are after or they are able to point you in the right direction. Both your own trade publications and the publications of peripheral trades and interest groups should serve you well. Groups, associations and guilds receive information all the time of what is happening within their range of interests; most of them print newsletters or magazines to which you can subscribe. Some of them take a much more active role with regard to education, selling, exhibiting, commissioning, etc. Information sought after, or otherwise, can come from the most unexpected quarter and it pays to be alert at all times to random knowledge that can be stored away and used at a later date. It is always a good idea to jot these things down in a note book lest they cannot be summoned from the far reaches of your brain in which they have been safely stored.

Applying research techniques to your own business can only be of benefit. Going back over periods of your work to discover what has been successful in the long term and where you have made errors of judgement. You may have always considered that it is the smaller items turning over quickly that have supplied you with the bulk of your income, only to discover on analysis that it is in fact the larger items with the slower turnover that are fulfilling this role. From your records you will be able to ascertain which selling outlets have been the most successful, from which events you have had most feedback or commissions. All of this information can be used objectively to enhance your working efficiency and prevent you from working under a false premise. It will serve as a constant evaluation and an objective assessment of whether or not your methods are working and indicate where adjustment may be necessary.

Research is another important tool, learn to use it wisely. All the indicators may advise you against a given path, but it may be a path you have always wanted to try, even if for only part of the way. While the research says it is inadvisable, it will also tell you what you have to lose or gain. In this way you will be able to make a judgement and travel the path if you so wish with your eyes wide open.

CHAPTER TEN

Lists and Indexes

Lists are not to be mocked, from your humble shopping list to the list of your creditors. Lists – retain information – focus the mind – put things in perspective – and into an order of priority. They are tools that like all others you must learn to use.

The most important list you will ever hold is that of your 'Prospective and Current Clients'. Never forget to enter the name and address of a customer or interested party on to the master list the moment they leave the premises. This sounds a little extreme, but it is worth that extra two minutes to ensure one hundred percent that the name, address and item purchased are not forgotten, or buried in the heap of paperwork on your desk. It is very easy for a customer to feel put out, or worse still offended, if you omit to invite them to a private viewing. It necessarily follows that, at best you may have lost a sale on that occasion, and at the other end of the scale you may have lost their patronage. Put like that – the two minutes adding them to the master list are well spent.

For private clients I would recommend index cards, on which you should write clearly and precisely so that you can read it next time you come to look at it. The information on this hand written or typed card is not subject to the Data Protection Act, but nevertheless, sensitive information is not part of what you need to know or should have any interest in keeping. Essential information would of course be the name and address; if you have been given Christian names make a note of them, you never know when you might need them. Always ask for the post code, it may not be forthcoming, but it is helpful to the Post Office to ensure safe delivery of invitations (remember you are always doing everything you can to stack the cards in your favour). Note down the date you first meet, this can be very useful if the people are seen to be interested in your work, but do not actually buy at the time. When, after a given number of years they still have not bought, you will know how long they have been on your list and will be able to make a sensible decision about whether or not to dispose of the card or try again this year. The date of purchases, the piece itself and the price paid are also essential information. I also like to add onto my cards any other information that is likely to prove useful in times to come, eg. birthdays, childrens' names and seemingly trivial information of this nature. You do not need to ask for it, just gather it quietly as and when you can. A birthday card or a get well card can be a useful public relations tool as well as giving pleasure.

My main reasons for recommending hand written index cards are twofold. They are very quick and easy to add to, even in the workshop; remember to keep a spare copy for safety, it would be catastrophic to lose it. The other far more important reason is that if you store the information in a computer, you may be tempted to print labels for invitations or other mailings. At the risk of repeating myself, everything must be special, a computer label is not. After you have consulted the up to date information on the Data Protection Act, put your clients into a computer listing by all means, this will ensure that you have more than one copy for safety – But please do not send them labels. If, on the other hand, your customers are wholesalers, buying and selling is merely a transaction to them and in these circumstances computer labels are reasonable.

If you sell very small items as well as larger ones, then obviously you will have to use your discretion as to whom to place on your 'Prospective and Current Clients' list.

Would that we could identify prospective clients. There are no rules. When the work costs hundreds and even thousands of pounds you would think that it would become easier. It doesn't. Some people will save to own something special and others are able to buy without a dent in their bank balance. Keep an open mind. During a conversation with people who are obviously interested in the work it can be beneficial to both parties to ask if they would like to receive further information, invitations to exhibitions, etc. and to mention that you have two lists, one for clients who wish to purchase and collect, and one for people who admire the work, to ensure that they do not miss an exhibition. People are generally honest and will say whether or not they would like to receive further information, and what kind they would like.

This second index I call 'Information Only'. It is an ideal place to keep one's friends and relatives who are not purchasers, and into which to move those who have never bought, but started in the customer file, or those who bought many years ago but have been unable to buy as your prices have increased. I feel that these customers should not be ignored; they bought when you were building your reputation, they believed in you and your work before you became established and deserve better than to be tossed aside. You may consider this sentimental clap-trap, but they are obviously great admirers of your work, their fortunes may change for the better, their enthusiasm may introduce a new customer.

Unless your relatives and friends are also customers do not put them on your client list. Private views are business affairs, for meeting customers old and new and selling work, not occasions where all your friends and relatives tell you how clever you are and drink all the profits while they are doing so. If you explain to them they will understand. Have a second occasion for them on another evening if you would like to, but you cannot afford for your attention to be diverted by the antics of your sister's new baby, or commiserating with your aunt over her neighbour's misfortunes, while a customer is trying to talk to you.

By the very nature of this file there can be few useful sources of names and addresses for your 'Prospective and Current Client' list. The most important one is of course the customers themselves and visitors to your premises who are interested but do not buy on that particular visit. Telephone and written enquiries can be sifted, as can visitors to exhibitions. One or two of your clients may suggest friends who would be interested in attending private views. People you meet in the course of your social activities may be worth consideration. Now and again the media may give you an idea, for example by publicizing a recent commission or sale at an exhibition, and thereby perhaps giving the name of an avid art/craft collector. With just a small amount of research you should be able to obtain the name and address for your own list.

You can buy lists. There are companies who specialise in holding and selling lists for a variety of purposes. I would strongly recommend that before you use one of these companies you find out exactly what you will get for your money; as with everything else, the cost and quality can vary enormously. There can of course be no guarantees of purchases. Building a good 'Prospective and Current Clients' can be a long slow process, so if you have not kept a record, or if you are newly started in the art/craft field begin your list immediately.

These very important lists must be constantly updated. If you have made a mistake and end up with obviously the wrong people at a private view, do not be afraid to change them on to the 'information only' file or to strike them off the lists completely.

As your 'Prospective and Current Clients' file grows its importance becomes much more significant. Buying art and craft work is not a national occupation. Only a small percentage of people buy good quality art and craft. From that small percentage an even smaller percentage would buy your particular product if they knew of it. To contact a tiny percentage of those buyers is extremely difficult and your 'Prospective and Current Clients' list is the only direct contact that you have with a fraction of that tiny percentage. Without your master list you are trying to achieve what the big companies are trying to do with large mail shots and Sunday magazine advertising – but without their resources. Their expectations are perhaps a one in a thousand response, you on the other hand are aiming and expecting to achieve a one in ten attendance at your private view, better if you can. Even this figure needs a mailing of 500 to produce fifty pairs (Mr. & Mrs.) of guests. Out of those, if again one in ten couples buy or commission that is five sales. These one in ten figures are a minimum to aim for. You can achieve, and should aim for, a better percentage. As you can see, the quality of your guest list is paramount, never underestimate its importance or neglect it.

Another important index you must build and maintain is that of media contacts and the guideline on how to collect these is given in the chapter on the media. These may be stored in a computer, not forgetting the current Data Protection Act regulations. If you are a great computer advocate, then it would be useful for you to pay the current fee for registration and comply with the legislation so that you may usefully store an index such as this on disc. Computer labels to the media are expected and acceptable.

Other indexes or lists that you may consider keeping are those of suppliers and other useful contacts for your work. Always ensure that these are well marked and not confused in any way. It may also be useful to retain the names and addresses of artists and craftsmen whose work you like; the time may come when you decide to organise an exhibition with others – this list will then be very valuable.

The notion of listing things can be very useful when it comes to working out the costs of any particular venture you may be embarking upon, whether it is the circulation of a press release, some research work, attending a craft fair or holding your own exhibition. Every item that you can possibly think of that will involve an expense should be listed. Stamps, photocopying, insurance, transport, new display material, absolutely everything connected with that particular project; in time you may have worked out master lists for various occasions. In this way you will know, give or take a small margin of error, what are the costs involved, and you will be able to make objective decisions about the viability or otherwise of your plans and the losses involved if your venture is unsuccessful.

Another useful list is that of requirements when working or exhibiting away from home. These lists should always be started several days before the event and be close to hand so that you can jot down further items you will need as they occur to you.

So far I have dealt with what I would call indexes or files, but now I would like to tackle one of the essential ways that I have of dealing with the problems of being self employed, feeling at times isolated, stagnant and even, periodically, in difficulties.

Have you never had so much work to do that you just freeze inside? A barrier comes down and you cannot actually do anything. That is the time to sit down quietly and list the many tasks ahead of you, along with the time they will take to do and deadlines, if any. Just this simple task will stop the panic. You will be able to put the items in order of priority and work out just how you are going to accomplish them. It may mean getting up earlier in the morning, or asking a friend or partner to assist with some of the more mundane tasks until the light at the end of the tunnel begins to appear. Such a small and simple task, but it is amazing how it will clarify things and give you an indication of how to manage your time and accomplish your work. Because the commitments have been going round and round in your head, they are no longer ten different requirements needing to be done within the next couple of weeks, but twenty or even thirty different time-consuming jobs that cannot possibly be accomplished in the next six months. When you write them down rationally and quietly it all falls back into perspective and you are able to undertake the work with a new efficiency and determination. Panic, the destructive element, has been eradicated.

There are other occasions when this simple operation of listing things can be beneficial in either illustrating that you have allowed your mind to develop a situation out of perspective, or that you have let things get out of hand, and corrective measures must be taken immediately. Whilst I would of course advocate a constant eye on one's financial matters, the ideal is not always adhered to, even in the best regulated workshops and studios. It does not alter the fact however, that you should keep a constantly updated list of your creditors and debtors, work in hand, when it will be finished and when you can expect either final or interim payments. Do not anticipate commissions before the deposit is received, nor the sale of a piece made speculatively, these should be considered as stock. This method will enable you to keep a constant eye on the financial situation and allow you to seek early remedies should things not flow as they are anticipated. You will be able to see which of your creditor's accounts must be paid as a matter of priority, and which you could delay for a week to allow you to finish and deliver your current commission, or send a reminder to a slow paying client. On the other hand you will also see when a celebration is called for.

When there are various options open to you for the coming year and you are not sure in which direction you should head to achieve your goal, again, sit down and make a list. Itemise the fors and againsts of each different option and what you anticipate they will achieve, this will clarify the situation and you will be able to make clear and objective decisions.

Sometimes, by the very nature of the working situations of self employed artists and craftsmen, it is not unusual to feel isolated, that others in your field are making it and you are not. In the workshop/studio on one's own it is not difficult to see how a small negative thought can catch you on a bad day and nibble away until it has become an all-consuming thought. Perhaps a customer has declined a commission, a rival has had significant press coverage, you have been turned down as an exhibitor at an exhibition. 'Big trees from little acorns grow', and negative thoughts are destructive thoughts. Do not let these feelings get out of hand, MAKE A CUP OF COFFEE AND A LIST. Just the thought of this autocratic command should bring some measure of a smile to your face as you down tools and do just that. Set down your accomplishments over the past year, and it must be all of them, no matter how trivial you feel they might be. Still practising your craft, keeping on top of the bills, satisfied clients, successfully won commissions, steps taken toward the master goal, they will be legion – write them down. Then list your objectives: what things are happening in the coming year, work to complete, exhibitions to take part in, commissions to win, etc. List the negative aspects of your work: being turned down for an exhibition, a rival's press coverage. Compare it to your objectives to ensure that you are dealing with them in your planning. This will give you solutions to solving the down side of things, you will also see that you have not been idle, that you have accomplished much and that slowly you will reach each of the intermediate steps allowing you to attain the goal you have set yourself (see chapter on goals/targets). The wallowing will cease and you will be able to carry on with your work with renewed vigour and purpose.

Keep your lists by you at all times so that you can refer to them, add to them as and when ideas occur to you, and when you have eliminated a negative or paid a big account that has been troubling you, strike them out and celebrate, even if it is only with another cup of coffee – a walk to the pub for a beer at lunchtime would be much more risqué.

I was once given a very sound piece of advice by a high-powered executive, 'Things are never truly as bad as they seem'. It is a well worn phrase, but when destructive thoughts are hammering in your brain it helps to know that, and it gives you the confidence to list the bills and the negatives, and to know that it cannot be as bad as you think. By keeping a constant eye on things in this way, you are not only ensuring that they are not allowed to get out of hand but you are looking for ways to turn them around.

CHAPTER ELEVEN

Communication

Communication covers a great deal of ground, from how your telephone is answered to the envelope your final account is sent in. It is another important opportunity for you to convey to your clients and business contacts that you are professional and attention is paid to every detail of every aspect of your business.

The telephone can sometimes be the first contact a prospective client has with you, therefore consideration should be given to your entry in your local (or area) directory. A simple one line entry is part of the service when a business line is installed, but you can choose under which heading it is placed. Give this a great deal of thought, remember one always gets the kind of clients that one caters for. If you are a furniture maker, but you place yourself in cabinetmakers or joiners, do not be surprised if you are continually contacted to make gates or hang doors. This applies to all fields of crafts. You may be a studio ceramist, but if your entry is under potter, you may receive enquiries from new restaurants for quotes for crockery. This can be a two-edged sword, because it can also be useful advertising space that, other than the set business line rental, you do not have to pay for. It is possible to have more than one entry, ie. under different categories, and it is possible to enlarge your entry and make it into more of an advert. It is also possible to have an entry, not only in your own area directory, but in surrounding area directories. Consider carefully, this entry will stay current for about two years and you will have to live with your decision.

There are no hard and fast rules for the way a telephone is answered. Politely and clearly is the general rule. There has to be a balance between a terse 'Yes' and the rapid but unintelligible 'McDonald, Wetherall, Sprockett & Jenkinson Associates, Amanda Jayne speaking. How may I help you?' The person at the other end of the telephone simple needs confirmation that he has reached the correct destination and the person he requires is close at hand or will ring him back. Listen with a critical ear to the way telephones are answered to you, and the way in which you respond to them, this will help to improve your own method of answering the phone. No one should answer your business line unless they are competent to take a clear and intelligent message or deal professionally with the enquiry. Harassed wives with fractious children should not be expected to answer the phone, nor should they. There can be very little worse than the sound of an irate mum with crying children at the other end of the line, except perhaps television or radio noise in the background.

Answerphones are useful tools and should not be abused. They are valuable if you are away from the studio or office, if you are doing something that cannot be interrupted, if you are talking to a client; it is bad manners and could well kill a sale if you neglect a client to answer the telephone. Zany outgoing messages are good fun on one's private line, but they are inappropriate for business. The outgoing message should be brief, confirm that the caller has reached the correct number, indicate when you will be available to answer the phone or return the call and request a message or the caller's details if the call is to be returned. The date and time can also be included if it is appropriate. CHECK YOUR MESSAGES AND RETURN ALL CALLS.

Likewise when you telephone a client, it is always useful to have jotted down the salient points of the object of your call (including your own telephone number and dialling code). In this way you will cover all the necessary points and if the client has employed an answerphone you will not sound tongue-tied as you leave your message. It would be inappropriate to leave messages of financial matters or details of their work that need further discussion.

Almost all other communication you will have with your client will be either in person, or on paper in one form or another, letters, quotations, accounts, sales literature, invitations to private views, brochures, etc. It is therefore important to ensure that the material you are using, ie. your printed stationery and promotional literature again reflect the attention to detail that the client can expect in your work.

Perhaps at this time you should decide if you are going to employ a logo. This is of course a personal choice; it may be as simple as the initials that you sign your work with, or something far more elaborate that you may feel is appropriate. A decision should also be made at this stage as to whether or not this logo should be included on the stationery

The heading for all of your paperwork should be uniform, in the interests of continuity, so that your paperwork is readily recognised by your clients, and you continue the persistent drip, drip, drip, on the metaphoric stones that are your prospective clients. It should also be clear, well designed and legible. Some 'arty' headings convey nothing but muddled thinking and a lack of good design. It is possible to strike a balance between the illegible 'arty' and the boring printed notepaper favoured by the 'professions'. You may feel that you can design it yourself or you may have seen some headed notepaper that you like which could be altered slightly for your purposes.

Some companies run a full design and print service which is reasonably priced. They will offer you various alternatives based on the information and preferences you have given them. Whilst it will cost you a little extra if you do not like their initial designs and ask for more to be prepared, it will be irksome to use stationery that you know could have been better and to change it at a later date will incur all of the origination costs again. Always check your proofs properly for the tiniest spelling mistake or wrongly placed number. You will be using the paper for a long time, it must be right, there will be no comeback on the printer if he has given you a proof and you haven't corrected it. Once the film is made, the second and subsequent runs will be less expensive.

It is always a good idea, before embarking on any printing that you anticipate using for an appreciable length of time, as with your entry in the area directory, that you check to ensure that your area code or telephone number are not due to be altered in any way. It can be annoying halfway through a consignment of stationery to be advised of a number change. The telephone company usually knows well in advance of any planned changes and will be able to advise you accordingly.

If cost is a consideration and you have spent your budget on the artwork and paper quality it is not necessary to have everything printed at once: for example, A4 paper, A5 paper for small notes , compliment slips, invoices and business cards – stick to the essentials: invoices, A4 note paper and business cards. If the invoices have the same size headings as the note paper, that will save money on the cost of origination. Liaison with the origination department will help in all ways of maintaining quality at minimum expense. If you have chosen a good firm, with a design capability, you will find that this will be less expensive than going to an agency and then to a printer.

Work at building a good working relationship with the printing company, so that you both understand how each other works. You will know what is expected of you by way of input and the standard of artwork necessary to produce good clear printing, and the printer will know the quality you expect. Choose carefully in the first instance and build on that relationship. It will pay off in many ways especially when you are doing exhibition catalogues, etc. and working to tight deadlines.

Your sales literature should be designed and commissioned with the same care as for your letterhead. A good working relationship with the printer will pay dividends here. You will be able to explain to him that you want the earth but can only pay with buttons. There are so many different papers, printing processes, finishes, etc. that only by being able to rely on your printer can you expect to be told what is available and what is possible. Having a brochure, or even a leaflet printed can be expensive and can produce such disappointing results if you are not careful. I can only give you guide lines, and these cannot provide for aesthetic considerations.

If the brochure is to contain photographs, the printer must be given a selection of the different grades of lighting, their scanners will read the photograph differently to the naked eye. The printer will know which one to use, it is their job. Having said that, if you are after a particular mood or shadow lighting, tell him what it is you are seeking. The photographs must be of superb quality.

You may have specific ideas about the layout, your printer may have a design service that you are using, or you may be using an agency. Nobody is infallible, if you do not like the ideas put forward, say so; it is better to alter them at this point than try to live with something you do not like. As with everything else, do some research, find brochures and leaflets that you do like, colour schemes that you feel would be appropriate. Make your own mock-ups, play about, experiment.

The text copy (the wording) is also important. Do not use the first person. There are rare occasions when this is appropriate, for example a quotation, but nothing sounds more amateurish or conceited. Write clearly, employing the who, why, what, where and when, to ensure you say all that you want. Try to eliminate ambiguities. If necessary get help, someone competent in writing, not necessarily 'arty'. Do not use 'Art speak' no matter how much you are tempted, it sounds like the emperor's new clothes to all but the academic psuedo artist – they talk about art, they do not buy it.

When your proof arrives look through it carefully. Most typesetting these days is done on a computer and sometimes it can be seen in large headings that the letter spacing is not as good as it could be. This is an obvious item to look for, but there are other much more subtle areas of the layout of the wording that separate the good jobs from the excellent. Hold your proofs up to the light to see if the letter lines and margins run together. Check carefully for spelling mistakes, word omissions and correct number formations. For the uninitiated the commissioning of a brochure or leaflet can be a minefield, but with a good printer they can be an excellent communicator of your work, and the standards you have set.

The method of commissioning sales literature and brochures will similarly apply to an exhibition catalogue if you require one. The only difference will be the content and deciding whether or not to put the prices in the text or employ a separate price list. Including the prices can have both advantages and disadvantages. The advantages are of course cost, but these are far outweighed by the disadvantages of having to know the full content of the exhibition so far in advance and possibly alienating members of the public to whom you cannot afford to give a free copy of the catalogue.

I like to send out a catalogue with each private view invitation, to give the client a glimpse of the new work, to encourage them to come along and see the pieces in the flesh. If they are unable to attend it keeps them abreast with what you are doing. It will also work for you in your absence, in that it will be shown to friends and colleagues and may well result in a request for an extra invitation for the colleague and who may become a new client. This being the case the artwork for the exhibition catalogue needs to go to the printer six to eight weeks before invitations are posted which can be three to four weeks before the exhibition. A maximum of twelve weeks before the exhibition, there is time still to add to the content of your exhibition. For this reason I favour a catalogue that contains only some of the work to be exhibited, and this is clearly stated in the catalogue, The price list, because it is all text, has a much quicker turn around at the printers and can be left until the almost last moment, approximately two weeks before the exhibition, when all participants should know all pieces and all prices. It is also an option to have the price list printed immediately prior to the posting of the invitations and include it with the brochure. This will depend on your own personal preference and the practicalities of the operation. It will contain all the pieces, descriptions, prices, etc. and can be given to your guests at the exhibition. Because of the lesser cost of the price list you can give these also to members of the public who visit after the private viewing, in this way they will have all the information necessary to enjoy the exhibition and can buy a catalogue if they so wish. Whilst it is reasonable to give expensive catalogues to your clients, it is not possible to give them to all visitors to an exhibition that may be open for a week. Some members of the public may be reluctant to pay for them, and by employing this method you eliminate pressure and possible ill-feeling.

The exhibition catalogue should of course 'hang together' with the invitation and price list and any other literature you are using such as postcards and posters for advanced publicity. A good way to do this is to choose early on the photograph to be used for the front of the catalogue, this should then be used for press releases, any advertising you may take and the posters and postcards if used. It should be obvious that all the literature refers to the same event. Therefore, each piece should not only contain the chosen illustration but also the name of the artist/craftsman, the exhibition and the venue. For example: Studio '96, an exhibition of the work of Andrew Jenkinson at The Priory. With regard to the catalogue text, this includes the names of the pieces illustrated and your name and address, and a telephone number for further information is essential. Other information you might consider including are; any acknowledgements due, a small item of text about yourself and your work (written in the third person), the sizes and materials used for the illustrated work, the dates and times of the exhibition, etc. It depends on how you envisage your catalogue and the work that you intend it to do for you. A5 is an excellent size, it is easily handled, yet big enough to be taken seriously, and good quality envelopes are readily available. Done correctly with a smart invitation it will make a very impressive piece of mail for opening.

Depending on how you see your exhibition catalogue and what you have included in the text, it may be appropriate for the printer to print more copies than you envisage using at the exhibition. It is also possible to have the extra copies overprinted with another venue or address. In this way you will have top quality sales literature to use for promotional purposes after the exhibition as well.

Invitations can come in all shapes, sizes and qualities. They should reflect once again the quality of your work, be a joy to receive, make the recipient feel that they have been especially requested to attend and be at home amongst the other important invitations your clients receive. Pay even more special attention to the invitations, there are no hard and fast rules as to how the wording should be laid out. Ask to see the examples that your printer will have, but always be aware that you can have a different card from the sample, a different size and a different typeface to match the one you have already chosen for the catalogue. To hand write the name of the recipient on the card shows that you have taken extra care, but do not write too many at a time so that your writing becomes tired. Some invitations have 'wine' printed at the bottom, personally I feel that this is unnecessary. What kind of a host is it, that invites people to travel to an event, possibly to spend money, and does not offer them refreshment? This word on the bottom of an invitation is not going to spur a client to attend for his free glass of wine.

R.S.V.P. is a difficult concept to decide upon. On the one hand you may need to know numbers, although at a private view this is unlikely unless more elaborate refreshments are planned, but it may make the invitation appear more important. On the down side, is one's client going to make a commitment weeks ahead for a private view, and if they do not R.S.V.P. do they then feel, on the night when they do decide to come, that they cannot because they did not reply? Sometimes in this business a crystal ball is an important tool, never more so than in the business of invitations to private views and how to ensure that they work. All that you can do, and must do, is stack every single, last, little card in your favour, cross your fingers, close your eyes and make a wish.

Advance publicity for an exhibition need not be expensive. With transfer letters (eg. Lettraset) and word processors it is possible to cut and paste an acceptable poster that will look impressive copied at the copy shop on a colour printer. Start with the size required, A4 will ensure more ready homes for your poster than anything bigger. Place your photograph and then the text at the top and bottom. Only fixing them when you are happy with the overall image. Care must be taken not to cast shadows with the edges of applied layers, special cellotape can be purchased for this purpose. For the computer literate a very good D.T.P. package may well prove useful.

For posters and postcards used you must be sure to include all necessary information; Who, what, where, when and how. If the venue is not easily located and is to be signposted by one of the motor associations this should be indicated. Ask a colleague to check the information for you, it is surprising how often vital information is omitted.

When writing letters headed notepaper must be used if you wish to appear professional and show that you mean business. Writing on ordinary paper is fine for a personal letter to relatives and friends, but not for any business purposes at all. A letter is a more tangible communication than a telephone call or a conversation. It can be held in the hand and studied, the impression it leaves depends on the attention you give it before you finally sign it and put it in the envelope. Having worked to get your notepaper right, you must continue the process of quality and learn how to set out a letter on a page. A wordprocessor is marvellous for this purpose, in that it tells you how long your letter is before it is printed and it is now easy to position the letter properly – for those of you with a typewriter it is a question of trial and error, but if the letter is important and ends up in the wrong place on the page, there is no other recourse but to retype it. Do not hand write a business letter, you may feel your hand writing is beautiful and this may be true, but this is business and it must be clear that you are a professional. Typewriters, and for that matter word processors, are no longer expensive and should be considered as an essential part of your equipment. No one but you will know how many fingers you have used. You can of course use a typing agency for your correspondence, your partner may be persuaded into helping you with these things, but many of you will in fact be doing this essential work yourselves in the evenings and at weekends.

Now to the actual wording: work on the who, what, when and where principle, and make your letter clear, precise and to the point. Don't waffle, no one wants to read it. English has never been my forte and I'd be the last to advise about the grammar of your letters, suffice to say they must flow easily with no obvious bad grammar. Draft your letter first, read it through and correct it where necessary and then do it for real. This will also help with positioning your letter on the page. Don't guess at spelling – look it up.

Make sure you spell the names and addresses correctly and that you give the recipients their correct title, Mr, Mrs, Esq., Lord and Lady, Dr, etc. If you are unsure how to address a dignitary you will find the staff in reference libraries most helpful. There are also reference books, such as Burke's Peerage, where you will find this type of information. These minor details may be a bore but this letter may be the only communication you have with a prospective client, sponsor, etc. and the way you present your case may determine whether or not your epistle goes in the bin, in the file, or onto the desk for action. Getting peoples' names correct is a small common courtesy. How much better received your letter will be if it is addressed to D. A. Smith, Manager, Smiths Gallery, beginning Dear Mr Smith, rather than Manager, Smiths Gallery – Dear Sir or Madam. This information is readily available, just by using the telephone. One can usually obtain information like this from the secretary or receptionist. The recipient will know you have made an effort and appreciate it.

Always sign your letters with a good pen, this will make you hesitate and then sign the letter carefully. Do not use a cheap ball point, felt tipped pen, nor, unless you wish to project a particular image, a funny colour. The letter is important, not something you have knocked up and felt so unimportant that even your signature is a scrawl – a dismissal.

Sometimes you will receive a letter that disturbs you in some way, makes you angry, disappointed or aggrieved. Do not answer the letter and post your reply on the day of receipt. By all means dash off an angry response if it makes you feel better. Then in the cold clear light of the following day when you have slept on the problem, tear up your immediate response and answer the letter properly. You may be just as angry, but you will be better able to compose a thoughtful reply.

Invoices and quotations should have your terms printed on the bottom or reverse to hopefully avoid unpleasantness. It looks more professional if they are printed and it will not appear to be personal to your client as it would if you typed it separately on each invoice. It will be accepted as your terms and conditions, consistent for all your clients. These terms should include: methods of payment; for finished goods and work in progress, how long you are prepared to wait for payment; the fact that the goods will remain yours until paid for in full; who will pay for postage and packaging if that is applicable, etc. etc. Only you can decide your terms of business, but it would be wise to spend a little money to consult with your solicitor to ascertain what would be appropriate for your own particular business. It will save you money to be well prepared when you seek advice, ie. your methods of doing business and what eventualities you wish to guard against. He/she will be able to advise you what is and isn't possible and, with all things legal, the wording will be everything. There are solicitors who run schemes whereby you can consult them free for the first half an hour, but failing this how much better to expend some money at the beginning than to perhaps get embroiled in unpleasantness and legal costs in years to come trying to enforce unstated terms.

The same care must go into the preparation of your invoices and quotations as into your letters. Invoice pads are not a very good idea, because it is tempting to write them out and pull them off, rather than use the typewriter or word processor. Obviously, at exhibitions and fairs this is more difficult, in that case write clearly, do not scribble, and if appropriate follow up with a properly typed invoice.

The envelope your letter, invoice, quotation goes into is equally important, it is possible to have the paper of your stationery and envelopes to match, and this you must ensure when choosing the paper at the printers. If the contents of the envelopes are typed, then the envelope should be typed, but if it is an invitation then it should be hand written if you have a good hand. Never send computer labelled envelopes to your private clients, it smacks of a circular and not a piece of mail worth opening.

Business cards, although not seen as much now, are still a useful tool. A small handy card which should contain your name, address, telephone number, occupation, and if appropriate opening hours. There has been a tendency over the past few years for an illustrated postcard to replace the business card and it is debatable which serves the purpose more effectively. With the business card you are unable to illustrate the quality of your work, and have to let the business card intimate that for you. With the postcard comes the problem of size, in that they are too big to carry around in a wallet. The answer to this dilemma is that they both have separate roles to play. The business card fulfils the traditional, professional role of allowing someone to take away your name and address, should you wish them to, without scrambling about for a scrap of paper and writing it down usually in conditions that are not conducive to legible handwriting. The postcard allows you to illustrate one or more examples of your work for people to take away at craft fairs and other promotional activities. They can carry useful information on the reverse, for example open weekends or exhibitions. They can be used literally as postcards, in that you can have information printed on half of the reverse and put a name and address and a stamp on the other half. They can be cheaply produced by one of the many printers advertising this service in the trade press. The quality varies, so be sure to ask for samples before placing your order and do not be afraid to send faulty work back if it does not meet the standard of the samples. I would not advocate using them for an occasion that is important to you such as exhibition invitations. Regard them as memos; they have a role to play but should not be confused with a formal communication. Remember, if you decide to use postcards in this way that the photographs used for reproduction should be superb.

The price of your product is very important information which you have to communicate to your clients. Sticky labels are out. Remember that your work is special, you do not want it covered in goo. One only has to remember how annoying it is at Christmas trying to remove not only the labels, but the sticky residue left behind to reinforce this taboo. Neither should a display of one's work look like flag day with little cards on strings waving in the breeze.

For exhibitions, items should have a discreet numbering system. There are several different types commercially available in plastic, varying in both size and colour. It is also possible to have some made in wood, ceramic or stone, but do not use bent pieces of card on which you have written either numbers or descriptions. This numbering system enables you to compile a price list for your clients, giving not only the title, description and price of the piece, but also your logo, name, address, telephone number, opening hours and the fact that you accept commissions and would be happy to discuss them, if that is appropriate. It gives you the scope to wax lyrical about the piece, it makes the exhibition more interesting for the visitors and it is something for them to take home and refer to again if required. Price lists should preferably be printed on card or firm paper and should be A5 in size, this is to facilitate its use at a private view when your clients are also trying to juggle with a glass of refreshment. A photocopied piece of A4 is so easy to dismiss as trivial, it becomes an encumbrance because of its floppy nature and as part of the natural course of events it gets folded away into a pocket or handbag never to be referred to again.

If you have your own showroom you can employ this method of pricing, obviously it would have to be updated as you sold work and made new pieces. In this instance it would be acceptable to type your list onto your headed notepaper, A5 if you have some, and get it properly photocopied in appropriate numbers. If you only have A4 notepaper most photocopy shops do reductions.

If this method is impractical then you have no option but to have small cards beside your work. These should be kept to a minimum. Choose a good thick paper and type the information, try to keep them all the same size. Cards laid flat look better than bent cards at differing stages of collapse. Once again, it is possible to buy card holders, or to get some made. This has to be well worth the effort; a further display of your constant attention to detail and the regard that you yourself have for your work.

Touching can be a nightmare at most occasions. Childrens' wandering fingers while a parent's attention is elsewhere or a moment's thoughtlessness by a ring-wearing visitor. It all has to be guarded against, and this fact has to be communicated to your visitors. As with pricing, if you have to have a request not to touch prominently displayed on a card so be it, but if it is at all possible it should be more of a polite reminder in the price list. Watchful attendants are then able to draw attention to the request, possibly striking up a positive discussion with a prospective client at the same time. I feel here that it is important to remember, that unless you have placed your work in an inappropriate place then your work will only be touched by admiring clients and their children. Authoritative DO NOT TOUCH commands will alienate them whereas a gentle 'I know it is irresistible but . . .' may lead on to a good contact if not a sale. Exhibitions open to the general public will obviously need stronger reinforcement of this rule, and one well placed notice at the entrance to the exhibition backed up by the reminder in the price list and watchful attendants should do the trick. Now and again you will come across the persistent toucher, if not dismantler, and you will find yourself in a situation where it will be necessary to ask them to leave. This should be done as quietly and as calmly as possible with a refund of any entrance fee paid. You owe it to yourself, your clients and your visitors not to make any exceptions and allow a possible breakage because the perpetrator is persistent and ill-mannered. Unless they own the work they must respect the wishes of the owner – they have paid to look, not to touch.

Sometimes it is expedient to use a photocopier, as in the example of the price list, for a frequently altering showroom. However, you must ensure that only the best examples of the 'photocopiers art' are ever associated with your work. If you have access to a machine then it is possible to set it up properly so that it only prints good clear copies centred correctly on the page. If you are using copy shops they should only offer you good, clear, symmetrical copies. Do not accept anything less. Please do not offer your clients anything less.

Facsimile copies should only be used if circumstances dictate. Not circumstances of your making, ie. that you are late submitting a quotation, etc. but of the client's making. The fuzzy text on inferior paper is totally unable to convey any degree of quality whatsoever, the only thing it can convey is that you are late and must use this method because you did not get the paperwork in the post on time. If, however, the use of the fax is client driven then so be it.

Again and again during the course of promoting and marketing your work you will need photographs. This work can be expensive and disappointing. Professional photographers come in all shapes, sizes and cost and research has to be the key. You must ascertain what they normally photograph. The vast majority of them do weddings and portraits, most of the time you will be requiring the equivalent of a still life in art. This requires a studio, lighting and a photographer familiar with the subject, so ask to see some examples of his studio work. Then you must discover the absolute bottom line of the costs involved. Some will charge by the hour plus costs of film, developing and printing, others will charge per image: for example, x for the front view, x for the side view and so on. You must also discuss who will own the negatives at the end of the session; if it is the photographer you will be tied to him for all your work on that subject and paying his price for every print required. If he is good, he will be worth every penny and your work will sing off the celluloid, if not you will be very disappointed and there will probably be no comeback unless he has made glaring errors, such as having only half of the piece in focus or footprints on the backdrop.

You may decide to take the photographs yourself or ask a friend who enjoys photography to do it for you, perhaps you know a good competent amateur who will enjoy the challenge. Or there are a number of classes run by colleges and camera clubs who would be only to happy to accommodate you. In all of these less than professional activities your major cost will be film and developing rather than studio time and in this way more film will be expended trying to get the desired result. I would only advocate these methods if you are prepared to persist until you get the result you want, rather than one that 'will do'.

When deciding on the image you are seeking to portray with the photographs of your work I would suggest that you look through glossy magazines, good quality calendars and the excellent books of photographs available in bookshops. In this way you can determine whether or not you like directional lights, colour backgrounds, the whole or only part of the piece illustrated, a 'moody' image or a cold, clear one. This will enable you to show the photographer what you are looking for, or, if you are doing it yourself, show you which part in the many reference books on photography to look up to achieve a similar result.

If you decide to take the photographs yourself, or to have a friend do it for you, do be careful that at the end of the day you do not end up with amateur snapshots – for example your work in the garden with the children playing in the background, or your work on the television set with a proud Auntie May looking on. These are super for your private album, but not for business; no one will use them.

It is always expedient, whoever takes the photographs, to take black and white as well as colour slides, in this way you will have every option open to you; colour photographs, colour slides and black and white. Once you have paid for the studio time it is not necessary to have all the work processed to the end. The films can be developed, which for slides is the end of the line, and the black and white negatives can be transformed into a contact sheet for reference. The next step is to make either of them into a useable form, copy slides made from the very best shots, this will ensure that after a few mailings you are not searching amongst the 'also rans' to ascertain which is the least worst among them. But do remember to keep the master, you will always lose a little something copying a slide and therefore it follows that you will lose even more copying from a copy. For your own print work always supply the printer with an original. From the contact print you will be able to select the best of your black and white prints and have them processed to the required size. Always keep your photographs carefully, using a system which will make it easy to locate any particular one at any given time.

Having expended the time, energy and money on these photographs ensure they are correctly labelled (see Chapter 14) and that they are secure when you post them. There are special envelopes, into which you can introduce another piece of board to be absolutely sure, and there are plastic wallets for slides, again a little extra insurance. There is a debate about whether or not to use glass mounts, if these are damaged, in the post or otherwise, the glass will scratch the slide and make it unuseable. If card mounts are employed these can bend and again damage the slide. Plastic, re-useable mounts are perhaps the best bet, they pop shut and will pop open for use if required.

CHAPTER TWELVE

Sales Opportunities

When you are happy and confident with your work, then is the time to look for sales outlets, display areas and other ideas to put your work before prospective clients. These are many and varied, from building society windows, prestigious galleries, targeted sales opportunities, exhibitions, craft fairs, through to a small corner of your workshop. Those you choose to pursue will depend on which sector of the market you wish to target, which method is best suited to your product and the type of venue you wish to use. It is not necessarily the most obvious ideas that are the most beneficial. Be alert at all times to new and unusual potential sales and display possibilities.

When choosing venues for selling and showing your work always bear in mind the audience you are trying to appeal to with your work, where in the social structure the bulk of your clients fit. Bear this in mind all the time you are doing your research so that you are able to recognise good positions and opportunities to show your work.

I feel that the ideal outlet is one controlled by yourself. I have run The White Knight Gallery for twelve years now, the last nine exclusively for Ian Norbury, selling his wood sculptures. This has been to my mind the best way to sell the work of an individual.

With your own shop or gallery there are so many advantages. The work can be displayed, lit, looked after, kept clean and polished as you would want. Whilst it is my belief that good galleries would look after your pieces as you would yourself, I have attended good galleries with excellent reputations and seen the work of an acclaimed woodturner stacked like a pile of dirty dishes, and at another, covered in rain spots. With your own shop window, the public are able to look through the windows during the daytime and in the evenings. Clients and visitors are able to come in and look at the pieces without feeling obligated. If a sale is made, or seems likely, the customer is able to meet the artist/craftsman if they wish and to discuss the piece in greater depth. The maker's day remains uninterrupted unless something important happens; he is not at the beck and call of casual visitors. With one base and a growing international reputation people are able to locate and visit, confident of seeing all the work you have on offer. Your work is not being spread around a number of galleries leaving you with no representative collection in any one place. There is no middle man afraid of losing commission and wanting all dealings to be through him. This will be of benefit to both you and your client, because you are not keeping your prices artificially increased to make allowances for commission being added to your work at various other selling venues, and your client will know and appreciate that fact. You do not have to go treking around the country looking for suitable sales outlets. It can be very difficult to sell your own work to galleries and shops, intimidating to unpack one's work in a gallery and be turned down, no matter how kindly it is done or for whatever reasons, it can be a very harrowing experience. Everything points to having your own sales outlet as the ideal way of selling your work. Promotion and marketing become very important skills for you to acquire because you will not get the casual trade that one would experience in the middle of town. You will therefore need to make the public aware of you, your work and where you are.

There are disadvantages of course. A shop commands commercial rates, electricity, water and telephone. Those of you that make work from a garage or outhouse at home and keep a very low profile locally may only pay domestic charges for all of these things and may not even have planning permission, but when you buy a property with a shop or commercial workshop you will find the cost of the services very different. If the building is half domestic and half commercial it is termed 'mixed hereditament'. The rating office set the business rate and the water board add their share for good measure, and along with the telephone and electricity it is all considerably more expensive than the normal domestic charges.

You must find someone competent to run your gallery and undertake perhaps ten to sixteen hours' paperwork a week. If your partner is interested, or prepared to be interested that is ideal, otherwise you will have to pay someone, which isn't terribly clever as it is not a full time occupation, but someone needs to be on call as long as the door is open. Another alternative is to set up a bell so that when someone enters the shop you will know and can attend yourself; this may not always be convenient, depending on the type of work and volume of visitors you expect. It will interrupt the flow and concentration of your work, and whilst this may be agreeable for a sale it is not so agreeable if it is the third person that morning asking for directions. You could try opening on certain days, but that isn't terribly clever either if a prospective client is, for instance, on holiday in your area and decides to visit you, only to discover you're closed on that particular day.

If there are several of you wanting to sell your work, perhaps you could get together and employ someone between you, or take it in turns to man the shop. This second idea moves away slightly from the original concept, in that the craftsman is no longer on hand to discuss commissions or clinch a sale, but you are still in control of most aspects of selling your work.

Craft galleries can be excellent retail outlets for your work if they are well run and the owners and managers know their subject. The Crafts Council produce a leaflet with a list of galleries that they recommend. You may wish to use these as a starting point, but this is not all that is available by any means. Neither is it a comprehensive list of the only good outlets. It must be remembered that it is only the Craft Council's opinion of what they find acceptable of the galleries that approach them for recognition. There are craft shops and galleries in the market place as good as if not better than those listed by the Crafts Council who have never sought either their recognition or approval.

This being the case, you must look around. It is more feasible to start locally, spreading your net further afield as and when you feel it necessary. Go to these outlets as a customer, ascertain if they are helpful and knowledgeable. Whether or not the work is well looked after, well displayed and if the gallery is local, over a period of a few of months, you will be able to see if the work sells. During this period of research try to discover whether or not the gallery/craft shop in question has a good reputation, a programme of exhibitions and its financial stability. Ask yourself these important questions: 'Is this the right place for my pieces? Do they have the appropriate calibre of customers? Will they sell and promote my work?' Not just the age old question 'Will they take my work?' If it is not the appropriate venue with the correct market sector then it would be a waste of your time and their's to make a formal approach.

If you feel, after your researches, that this could indeed be a good place for your pieces and that the proprietor may well be interested in your work, go home and prepare your approach. The way you present yourself and your work is very important. The way not to approach any sales outlet can best be illustrated by the situation most recounted to me by craft shop and gallery owners, and certainly experienced by myself. That of the craftsman, arriving without a prior appointment, in working clothes, carrying a holdall, or even at times a plastic carrier bag, dropping workshop debris, if not mud from around the studio on the spotless carpet, denigrating the work on display as he passes. Emptying the contents of the bag on the floor or display area, discarding old towels and bits of newspaper into some semblance of a pile to reveal his pride and joy – his work. The irony of this situation is that the craftsman expects to be taken seriously, he feels that his work should be the only thing that he should be judged on. Not his timing, lack of manners, his appearance and worst of all the way he treats his work. If you do not treat your work as special – how can you expect anyone else to do so.

You will only have the one opportunity, if your work is rejected you may not feel able to make another approach. So, do it properly, stack the cards in your favour. For all the reasons mentioned above it is better in the first instance to write. You can convey more with a good clear letter, enclosing a C.V. and good, crisp, colour photographs than you can on the telephone. (Refer to Chapter 11). The recipient will be able to read, study and inwardly digest your efforts before making any commitment. He or she will need to be assured not only of the quality of your work, but of your professionalism. Many factors will come into the equation: whether your work is appropriate, will complement the other work carried or will be in direct competition with it. It will be reasonable if after a week or so you have not received a reply to your missive to telephone and make enquiries.

Most makers tend to look only to galleries and craft shops as a means of marketing their work. There are many various opportunities and differing venues from which to sell and display your work. The more of the correct market sector that see your work, the more likely you are to reach the even smaller percentage of that sector who will like it and the even smaller minority who will actually buy it. With all of these sales outlets and display areas your research and approach must be thorough. Sometimes the questions to be asked will be slightly different as will the contractual paperwork. When you have found a gallery, craft shop, retail outlet, display area, fair or exhibition be sure to work with the managers, organisers or proprietor for the mutual benefit of yourself, the outlet and the customers.

As you read this chapter I hope that ideas will come to you of venues in your area, or avenues you have not pursued to enhance the sales ability of your venture.

There are in every city, town and village, other shops apart from galleries and craft shops. Normally, the big chain stores have a central buying system, if you are a large producer you may wish to consider an approach, but do not be surprised if they require a large volume order. However, some of them allow their managers an element of local autonomy and a well prepared approach may prove fruitful to both parties. Your work does not necessarily have to be the same as that which they are selling, such as textiles in a shop specialising in fabrics, ceramics in a china shop, etc. It can be complementary or even perhaps a contrast to the normal products displayed. The following three examples show that this can and indeed does happen to the mutual benefit of both parties and will encourage you to think around the idea as it applies to you.

A colleague of mine, who sells furniture in a secondary shopping area, was able to place some of his pieces in the window of a well known chain store in what is probably one of the most prestigious, provincial shopping areas in England. This window was normally used to display soft furnishing fabrics. The furniture was used to great effect, and my colleague was able to place a promotional placard with his goods. The chain in turn were able to promote their fabrics and literature from his showroom window. The venue had been carefully chosen not only for the fabric to complement the furniture, but also for the furniture to complement the fabric. Both parties operate from the same town, and were able to envisage the promotional possibilities on offer of a cross pollination of clients.

In New Zealand, near Wellington, there is a very large, out of town cheese shop and they stock all the known local cheeses. It is a must for all visitors, and I was no exception. It was not a tasteless tourist trap, but a large airy shop full of delicious and tempting produce, set on a beautiful hillside with a superb restaurant. There amongst the cheeses were carved and turned cheeseboards made from every type of native New Zealand timbers. They were not fantastic examples of the makers' art, but they were competently made and placed in exactly the right spot for marketing. Just the right size and price to take home from holiday as a souvenir or a gift. So obvious when you see them in place – but perhaps a little lateral thinking suggested it in the first place.

Apart from mutual promotion and sales, there can be other reasons why a shop may display your work, it may be purely for altruistic reasons and perhaps to mop up a little publicity into the bargain. This was the experience of a national craft association who set up a travelling exhibition of carved animals in danger of extinction. The exhibition travelled all over the U.K. raising money for the World Wide Fund for Nature, and one of its venues was a chain store. There was no exchange of money, the exhibition was well attended and promoted in the local press. Not only did the chain store do a good turn for the association in hosting the exhibition, but they were also seen to be promoting human endeavour and the cause of the animals. They also received a bit of positive free publicity in the local press and who knows, perhaps some of the visitors to the exhibition bought something on their way out.

Smaller chains of the more trendy design orientated products are also reasonable retail outlets to approach, particularly if you work in small batch runs or even larger quantities. Some of these outlets may buy or commission as they would from a factory or wholesaler, but your research and approach should be none the less thorough, although perhaps less personal. Your work may not quite fit in with the retailer's own perception of the image that the shop wishes to project and suggestions may be made as to how your product could be altered to fit in with this image. If this is something you would wish to do, be aware that the retailer has assisted you in making a more saleable product and you have assisted them with the initial idea. Your contractual paperwork must reflect this to offer both parties mutual protection, ie. that you will not make this exclusive product for anyone else, and the store will not seek another craftsman to carry out the work.

You may consider the use of an agent. If you do, your research is of paramount importance. Think carefully around the subject. What will the commission be? When will you be paid: when the goods are taken, when the agent is paid, or a certain length of time afterwards? What happens if the client does not accept the piece? Many wealthy foreign families use agents. This could mean your work has gone abroad before you have been paid in full. Please do your homework very carefully. Do not be afraid to ask pertinent questions? List any that may trouble you and ensure you are happy with the answers. Read carefully any contractual agreements you may be asked to sign. I am not advocating that you do not use an agent; I know of craftsmen with very happy and fruitful relationships with agents, but I know of others with less happy stories to tell. Just be careful.

In the High Streets of towns and cities there are banks and building societies – opportunities to get your work seen by shoppers and passers-by all day and all evening when the lights are on. Managers are usually quite amenable to an approach from a maker wishing to display their wares, they are all too aware of how uninteresting their windows can be. Your display will encourage people who have long since ceased to notice the premises to stop and look through the window and it is good for their image to be seen to be promoting a local craftsman. Whilst this may be seen to be more of a display area, it does not necessarily preclude sales. This aspect of the arrangement should be discussed with the manager after a successful approach has been made. Sometimes popping a small item in a bag and taking money on your behalf may be seen as an extra service to the customers, on the other hand the staff may well already be very busy and unable to add this task to their daily work load and it may not be appropriate for your work. In your own interests you should make all enquiries easily answerable. Your name, address and telephone number, with a very short description of the service you provide, should be placed prominently in the window. Business cards or leaflets should be easily accessible for prospective clients to take away and perhaps a price list for the pieces displayed should be available with the leaflet. In this way you have done everything you can to facilitate enquiries and sales. Having secured an opportunity to display your work in this manner, do not forget the little touches; should you go and dust every day? – who will water or change the flowers? Do not forget that if a member of staff does sell a piece on your behalf, that there is nothing in it for them. A small token of your appreciation will not go amiss and it is good P.R. All these things must be thought through and catered for.

Another such display-cum-sales area is that of the hotel showcase. This will be a monetary transaction, but I feel for all that the research and approach must be as carefully prepared as previously. You will need to assure the manager of the hotel, or whoever is in charge of the display cases, that you are going to maintain the standards that have been set. You may well have to wait until an existing rental arrangement expires before you are able to take space, so if you are planning a big promotion for Christmas, or any other event, be sure you are planning a long way ahead. Sales may be considered part of the service to hotel residents, busy businessmen and women whose days and evenings are filled with meetings and formal dinners, who want to take home a gift for their partner, friend or relation, but know they are not going to see the outside of the hotel, let alone go shopping. Whether or not this is the case, once again you must make all queries easily answerable following the guidelines laid out in the previous paragraph. Remember, again, that it will probably be your responsibility to keep the display clean and attractive. The receptionists can be great allies, let them know that they are appreciated.

There are now many different qualities of craft fair catering for every market segment of the population, unfortunately there are more poorer than better quality ones. You will find information about them, ie. their timetable of venues and how to take part in your trade and associated interests publications. I cannot stress enough that you must do your research. If the craft fair you wish to participate in is away from home do remember in your costings to allow for travel, overnight accommodation and eating. Do not book a stand with an organiser whose events you have not attended. I know that this could mean a delay, but better a delay than wasted money and time, to say nothing of bad feelings you will have if you involve yourself and your work with something that you feel is second rate. Some of the better quality art and craft fairs only take place once a year and have a selection procedure and a long waiting list. If you would like to take part in one or more of them then the sooner you begin your homework the better. For the fairs with selection procedures you will normally be told how to apply and what paperwork and photographs are required. Do not forget to do it properly. You must also carefully read through your booking contract. Some organisers require only the booking fee, another may require also a percentage of sales and others might specify that all payments to be made to them and that you will be reimbursed after a period of time. There may also be hidden costs that you had not considered, lighting, hire of table, chair, etc. There may also be other clauses that you are not one hundred percent happy with; be sure none of these rules, regulations or costs take you by surprise. When you have successfully gained your booking at your chosen event you may well be asked which of the available stands or pitches you would like. Study the plan carefully, having due regard to the size of the area you will require and the cost, where the entrance, exit, competition, refreshments and toilets are positioned and the way in which they will affect sales of your particular product. Plan your display carefully and make the whole feel of your stand special. On the day, take care to strike the right note with your appearance, be cheerful and attentive. Do not eat on your stand, it looks dreadful. You will have seen during your tours of the various craft fairs what to avoid – eating, drinking, chatting to another stall holder while a customer is seeking attention, reading a book, looking bored and fed up, etc. etc – make sure you are not guilty of the same indifference to your prospective customers.

It is now commonplace to see craft areas within larger events such as the big agricultural shows, national festivals, hobbyist exhibitions, local promotional exhibitions, and race meetings, where the craftsman is able to benefit from the attendance of many thousands of visitors. The source of information for these varied events will be from local councils, reference libraries and the trade press of the initial instigators of the events. The whole experience will be similar to a fair devoted solely to crafts but with a larger through-put of visitors.

Trade fairs are a slightly different proposition. They are designed for wholesalers to display and sell direct to retailers. There are specialist, national and international events, and only by thorough research will you determine which one, if any, is appropriate for you. Most trade buyers will expect large quantities of identical items to very tight deadlines. Is this the type of work you want and do you have the capacity to produce it? If you do decide to take part in one of the very large trade fairs pay careful attention to your positioning, busy buyers are unlikely to visit every corner of the event. Trade fairs can be very expensive to take part in and it would be prudent to establish during your researches what type of buyer attends and whether or not the general public are admitted.

At any of these events, you should not rule out the possibility of exhibiting with other makers, sharing the costs, time and duties with colleagues. This could enable you to take a bigger stand at a more prestigious event and make a more eye-catching display. If you do decide to do this make yourselves a few basic rules of the division of labour, duties and costs at the outset to avoid any ill-feeling and to ensure the success of your endeavour.

Exhibitions can be superb events for sales, commissions and promotion generally. How to organise your own is dealt with in Chapter 13, but it is possible to take part in exhibitions organised by others. If your work is placed with a gallery they may well have exhibitions in which you may be invited to take part. When you are doing the research specified in Chapter 4 you may visit exhibitions in which you would like your work to be considered for inclusion. Through the press, by word of mouth, following motoring association signposts, in many different ways exhibitions may come to your attention. Do not feel inhibited; if you feel that your work would be appropriate, and everything that you have learnt about the exhibition is good and positive make a proper approach to the organiser. It may be that the exhibitions are not regular events, but do not allow that to dissuade you from making an approach, for if you are successful you know that you will be considered next time.

Slide indexes and registers are a dubious method of finding work. They depend on being properly selective, kept absolutely updated, competently cross referenced and well known about in the market place as a source of good quality and reliable makers. If you feel that you would like to be included in this method of marketing first ensure that your research and approach are properly carried out, then be certain to update your slides and entry regularly.

There is much ill-informed enthusiasm for selling abroad, and it must be admitted that in some other countries makers and their work are more highly regarded and sought after than in the U.K. All the above methods will in the long term attract customers who live abroad, but to establish a market abroad will cost large amounts of money, time, energy and commitment. I would suggest that unless you have explored every avenue at home and have a good solid business with excess capacity it is unnecessary to cast your net so far afield. We are all told from time to time 'take your work abroad, you will have no trouble selling it there'. The grass is always greener somewhere else, but you will know from experience that this is not necessarily true. Before you move one step further than considering trying to build a market abroad ask yourself whether or not you could improve your market at home by spending the same amount of money, time, energy and commitment. Consider the added burdens of transportation, customs documentation, guaranteed payment and packaging, to name but a few. If you are determined, there are various different schemes supported by the government to help you attend fairs and exhibitions in other countries. Starting points for your researches would be your own trade press, publications dealing with similar interests, national guilds and associations, the reference library, the Department of Trade, your local Member of the European Parliament and talking to people who have already tried it.

Competitions are yet another way of possibly attracting sales and commissions. To find out when and where competitions are taking place keep yourself well informed of what is happening in and around your field of work. Some competitions will be prestigious and others not, they will all require much work on your part and perhaps for little or no reward. You must decide for yourself the merits of each competition and whether or not you would like to take part. Bear in mind that although it is excellent to win a competition, it is not very good for your reputation or your self esteem if you lose.

You and your work should be registered with as many as possible of the commercial and government bodies that could possibly be useful to you: interior designers, architects, developers, builders, churches, insurance companies, restoration companies, the government Property Services Agency, the National Trust, and so on. You will be able to locate those more pertinent to your own craft by carefully thinking around the idea and applying a little research. In this way it is possible that when a craftsman is needed for a particular job you may be approached.

You might also consider tendering for work. This is the process of submitting costs for work along with other makers in your field for the customer to choose which tender he will accept. Sometimes the tender will be specific and the design, materials, etc laid out, in which case you will be asked for a price and a time frame. Other tenders will ask for designs and suggested materials as well. Many craftsmen obtain some of their work in this way. To obtain work like this it is important, not only to read trade publications in which some of them will be advertised, but also to be registered with trade agencies, guilds and associations. The more bodies that have details of the type of work you do the more likely you are to be asked to tender. Commissions of this nature can range from supplying a cafe or restaurant with crockery, cutlery or table linen, a company with new boardroom furniture, to a piece of sculpture for a hotel foyer.

Many guilds and associations, both local and national, hold exhibitions, craft fairs and other promotional events. Again, you must find those appropriate for you from your trade press and the local reference library. Some of them will have selection procedures and it is important to discover the criteria for admittance and whether or not you qualify before making an approach.

Direct mailings can work, it will depend on the type of work you do, the quality of your promotional literature and the quality of the list of names and addresses you are using. Large mail order firms do it all of the time, but they expect a smaller rate of return per thousand than you will, they have far more resources than you do and usually mail from tried and tested lists. If you intend to target a particular industry because you feel that you have something in which they would be interested, or you wish to be retained on their register, then direct mailing will be very useful. A mail shot of your new catalogue to your existing and prospective clients could also prove fruitful.

Advertising is another method of attracting sales. The old adage is that only ten percent of advertising works, but no one has yet been able to identify which ten percent. Certainly for an exhibition or an open weekend you will need to carefully place some advertising where your prospective clients (you will of course have invited your existing clients) will see it. If you are lucky the magazine will also give you a little editorial as encouragement for you to place the advertising, it is always wise to ask. Only you can decide if you are able to budget for advertising, but if you use it do try to monitor it. Ask new clients how they came to learn about you, this will help you to know if the advertising is worth the cost or indicate which of your other methods of attracting sales is working.

Local authorities are not renowned for spending money on art and craft, but it has been known, and it can do no harm to ensure that they know of you and your field of activity. Keep an eye on the local paper, and if it appears that they are considering something in which you feel you could well be involved, do not be shy. Find out who is in charge and make an approach. You may have an idea of your own to enhance something that the council is building or overseeing, such as a sculpture to commemorate the town's centenary in the new shopping arcade or a park currently being planned or built. Someone gets this work: with the right idea and approach it could be you.

This type of approach could also be undertaken with new office blocks, hotels etc. that are being built all of the time. Someone is responsible for the interior decor, fixtures and fittings. Find out who they are, make a well presented approach, and you could secure for yourself not only part of that project, but a good contact for work in the future.

There are now a few auctions for contemporary crafts run by one or two of the auction houses and you may like to consider this avenue for new sales. Be sure to read through your contract carefully, so that you know all the terms, conditions and costs involved. Do your research and be sure to find out how successful these auctions have been in the past.

Word of mouth is a super way to gain a new customer. It means you are getting there, that you are doing the right things. Continue to improve everything you do a little bit every day and it will ensure more clients by this method.

It is very important, that no matter which method or methods of selling and displaying your work you use, it is inevitable that you will receive clients into your workshop at some time or another. If you do not have your own showroom on your premises then you must consider devoting an area to the storage and display of newly finished commissions and the odd speculative piece you may have waiting to be delivered to a gallery. How much more professional this will appear to the client when he comes to look at his newly completed commission or drops in on the off-chance that you have something new to show him. Look around your premises with this in mind and if it is feasible do it.

If your premises are too small to display pieces awaiting delivery or collection then you must consider what you would do in the event of a visit from a client. It may be that you can arrange a display area which can be easily dismantled for just such occasions. This can be simply a roll of neutral coloured fabric or paper fixed to the wall above the bench and a spot light, or it could of course be more elaborate. One should not overlook the possibility of a potential sale in the workshop/studio.

CHAPTER THIRTEEN

Organising Your Own Exhibition

There are many reasons why makers should consider either taking part in or holding their own exhibition. Planned and organised properly with the right venue, right work and right atmosphere it is possible to sell a year's output at the private viewing. That is not to say that this will happen every time, but it is possible and something to aim for. They must be considered as selling events, not a time for people to slap you on the back and tell you how good you are. Praise will not pay the bills. They are a superb opportunity for your work to be seen by a wider audience, rather than just the maker and the purchaser. Sometimes one's work goes straight from the workshop into the home of a client, never to be seen by the public at large. An annual or regular event is an ideal way of keeping in constant touch with your clients and attracting new ones. They present the opportunity to seek publicity through the media and, done properly, can only help to enhance your reputation.

To organise your own exhibition is an enormous undertaking that should not be taken lightly. It is a tremendous commitment of money, time and hard work. It requires singleness of purpose, much planning and not a little courage.

Exhibitions by their very nature should be your best work. Not the table you gave to your mother when you left college, polished up a bit, but your most recent work, the very best of your ability. I cannot emphasise enough how important it is that the exhibits should be of the finest quality. You are putting your reputation on the line. The exhibition is going to cost a lot in more ways than one and you will be failing yourself if the pieces are in any way inferior. Imagine the scenario; it is your private view and you know that something is not as it should be. How can you confidently stand beside your work, glass in one hand, chatting to a customer who is thinking of buying it? How can you put your heart and soul into telling him how you made it, what materials you have used, explaining the design and the thinking behind it, when all the time you are hoping he doesn't notice this or that fault, or whatever else it may be you may have to hide? Everything at the private view and throughout the rest of the exhibition has to be working on your side. You are saying 'This is me! This is my work! For me to eat, you (the customer) have to like it, have to buy or commission.' It is a big ego trip and to my mind a necessary part of your calendar. You must do everything in your power to make it right, to make it special – starting with the work – your best work – from the drawing board to the last flick with the duster on the day!

Having decided to have an exhibition you should decide whether or not you are going to do the whole thing on your own or involve other makers. If you settle on the joint venture you must next decide if the exhibition is to be specialized, ie. all textiles, jewellery or ceramics or if it is to be a complementary mixture from several different fields. Then you must choose makers whose work is complementary to each other and not in direct competition. It must also be of the same standard you have set for yourself.

Sharing an exhibition can relieve the financial pressure enormously, but remember, you will still be doing the bulk of the organisational work, your time must be paid for. Bear this in mind when working out your costings. Great care must be taken in working out the finances for an exhibition. Make a list of every conceivable item that will be involved in the arrangements and the cost of each one, from the initial information sheet, the telephone calls through to the cost of the venue, the refreshments for the private view, printing, flowers and so on. In this way you will know what your budget is. You can decide how you intend to finance the event, and whether or not to invite other participants.

If you are going to work in this way with other makers and artists you must have a good clear set of rules and regulations which your participants will read and sign when they agree to take part and pay their fees. When others are involved it is only by this strict adherence to detail that the venture will be a success. Be sure that those you choose to join you are as committed to the success of the venture as you are. Your contract will be useless on the eve of the private view if only 75% of the work turns up. These rules should include:

> The fee and when it is to be paid.
> That if the work is not up to standard it will be rejected.
> Number of pieces to be exhibited.
> A date by which photographs will be submitted for press releases and other publicity.
> A date by which all work will be identified, with sizes, so that an initial floor plan can be worked out.
> A date by which all pieces will be named, with price and material used, for the catalogue.
> A commitment that only present and prospective customers will be

invited to the private view. No friends and relatives unless they are
clients.

A dress code for the private view.

An agreement to deliver and take away work as deemed necessary at
the time of the exhibition.

Method of payment during the exhibition, to whom the cheques will be
made payable and when settlement will be made.

As you can see from the above list an exhibition has to be planned like a military
operation. I look upon it as a train journey, with the decision to hold the
exhibition as the starting point, and the exhibition itself as the final destination. Along the route are signals for things to be done, and when you reach
them you must do them – don't procrastinate – do them. The success of the
exhibition depends on it.

You begin by working out the timing, several different factors will have to be
considered and this will ultimately help you decide when to hold it.

If all the work is to be for sale, then this is a massive undertaking and the time
factor should allow for money to be earned whilst preparations take place,
unless there is capital or resources to draw on. There are varying thoughts
about whether or not all work should be for sale and for the majority of makers
I feel that it should. As your reputation grows, clients will wait for exhibitions
in order to choose from more than the five or six pieces which may be your
usual stock. Many visitors will travel some distance and may feel justifiably
aggrieved if all the best pieces are sold and not available to them. For more
prolific makers of smaller pieces this will not be a problem, but for those of you
making fewer, larger items it is of course more difficult. Makers who work
mainly to commission would generally use an exhibition to show clients what
they are capable of, encouraging them to have the confidence to place an order.
Some clients may be reluctant to return work for exhibitions, they may feel that
the piece could be vulnerable both during transit and on public display. You
must make these judgements yourself. However you decide, all these factors
affect your timing.

How many pieces constitute an exhibition? Another factor to assist in
determining the timing. Whether or not the exhibition is solely for your own
work or to be shared with other craftsmen will help you to decide this number,
as will the final decision about the venue. With a conglomeration of diverse
makers, for example, a potter, a furniture maker, a rug weaver and a sculptor,
it may not make sense to have equal numbers of pieces from each participant.

Having thought carefully about the number of pieces to be exhibited and
whether or not they should be examples of work available, for sale or both, will
facilitate knowing how far in the future the event can reasonably take place.

Exhibitions should not be hurried; there is too much preparation to do to ensure their success. Neither should they be too far ahead as this allows complacency and a diminution of enthusiastic purpose. For the purposes of this book I am now going to use what I feel is the most effective lead time, that of one year.

The date and the venue are the next items to be considered, and they must remain independently flexible until both are established. The ideal venue may not be available on the favoured dates or for the length of time wanted, but the suitability of the venue may outweigh some of the considerations with the date.

The run up to Christmas is a good time, say September and October, after the holiday period with the festive season on the horizon. An ideal opportunity for clients to choose or commission gifts with enough time for you to complete the order and deliver the work.

January and February are perhaps the months to be avoided. It is a well known fact that the retail world goes very quiet at this time of the year.

The summer months of July and August give a mixture of signals. Both public and state schools are in recess, and it is generally the time of holidays. Having said that, many exhibitions are held at this time of year with varying degrees of success. Advance publicity and posters could well bring in new clients in the form of tourists staying in the area.

Other elements that may effect your dates are of more national concern. General elections, royal weddings, babies and special anniversaries will all divert the press away from the mundane items that normally fill our newspapers and magazines and make it that much more difficult to get press coverage. One should endeavour to find out when all the big events are scheduled and avoid them. Some things are, of course, beyond the powers of prediction.

Take an all-over view of the period during which you wish to hold your exhibition, and choose objectively. Again for the purposes of the book I have chosen what I consider to be ideal exhibition months, those of September and October. Now we have a sample to work with, an exhibition that will take place in September or October in one year's time. Firm dates have still to be established as does the duration of the exhibition.

One week, two, just three days, or maybe a month. The venue, and whether or not the exhibition is to be a shared event will be the deciding factors here.

The ideal venue must have the quality that you would wish your work to be associated with. It should be easy to find, have no traffic hazards and good clear parking areas if possible. Space for what you need, obviously more space is required for the private view than other days. Toilets if possible, a place to put wet umbrellas and raincoats, especially for the private view. A telephone for emergencies. It must be secure: different venues will have their own security problems – meet them realistically and solve them. Flooring must be looked at to ensure that none of your clients are going to fall flat on their faces. Where are the electric sockets? Look at the available lighting; is there provision for extra lighting? What is on the walls? Will you be able to take down what is there? Are there hanging facilities for your purposes? Should an artist or a maker of wall coverings be asked to join the participants to enhance the display? What pot plants are about? Will they improve the exhibition; will you bring your own?

Venues are many and varied, depending again on many factors. If five furniture makers are each to exhibit ten pieces of furniture you don't need to be a genius to work out that you need space enough for fifty pieces of furniture, as well as your private view guests, and room to move. How can they buy what they cannot see? On the other hand, one ceramist holding a one-man show of his wares will not need as much space.

A good local gallery could be a suitable venue. It will be possible during the initial research to ascertain if they have undertaken similar events before, the quality of previous invitations, posters, handouts and catalogues or price lists. There will be the added advantage of an established guest list for the private view. It is unlikely that a gallery would undertake an event like this if they were uncertain of the success of the venture. Their expenses, like your's, will be in advance of the event. It is imperative that you work with the gallery owner. Everything must be discussed and settled in the early stages of the arrangements to avoid any misunderstanding or unpleasantness. The division of labour and commission must be completely agreed upon. Galleries usually foot the bill of all expenses in exchange for a commission: 30–50% is about average. This is reasonable if the gallery is going to work hard on your behalf. Confirm in writing what has been agreed so that again no misunderstandings arise.

Do not be put off if the gallery has not hosted an exhibition before. If it has a good reputation , you can be sure that everything will be done to ensure the success of the venture. From their point of view it will be looked upon as a way to make money, of keeping in touch with their clients and enhancing their reputation.

Having decided to do it this way, do everything in your power to make it a success. If you have had press coverage, ensure that the gallery owner/ organiser knows so that the particular journalist will be included in the press release circulation. Make sure that an up-to-date interesting résumé of your life, (not a dull, boring list as per the normal c.v., or a long meaningless essay), and good black and white photographs and colour transparencies are available. Above all, be reliable. If an arrangement is made for you to be interviewed by the press as part of the run up to the exhibition, be there and on time. If you have said there is to be a wall-hanging in the rarest silks, make sure it is there. It will be meaningless on the day arriving without the wall-hanging saying 'there is a shortage of this rare silk'. A client may have travelled a long distance to buy it.

If you are seen to let people down they will not have the confidence to order from you and the gallery owners will not have the confidence to accept commissions on your behalf. Ultimately, the only person you let down is yourself.

If you choose to do your exhibition this way, your administrative load will indeed be lighter, but you must work with the gallery to ensure its success. Some of the points raised for those organising their own exhibitions may also be relevant to you.

It is possible to hire gallery and art/craft exhibition space, some may be staffed and others not. A good source of information for these venues would be the advertising section of art and craft orientated magazines and the book listed in the Bibliography "Directory of Exhibition Spaces". Do your homework carefully to ensure that the venue meets all your requirements and that you are happy with the terms, conditions and fee.

Hotels with conference facilities are another source of venue. These can be very costly, but it would also be prestigious to hold your exhibition in the best hotel in town. Some of the hotels have recently tarnished their image by holding bankruptcy stock clearance sales. Holding your exhibition in a hotel may persuade you to move your exhibition back into the holiday months when the hotel is at its busiest, particularly if it is to continue for several days after the private view.

Look carefully at the facilities on offer for an exhibition. You will find everything will be geared for a large influx of the general public, more so than the other venues discussed; toilets, food and the bar are a bonus. This will be purely a business transaction with set tariffs for a daily cost of the room/rooms involved. There will be terms and conditions which should be read through carefully, one of which will be a deposit, payable in advance. An entrance fee could be considered to offset this and some of the other costs involved.

One may not necessarily have to pay for the hire of the venue. If you are a good reliable craftsman it will be seen as good P. R. for a firm to be seen to be giving you a helping hand. Many companies have their hands tied with regard to cash, but are very approachable when it comes to space. You will have the added benefit of putting the directors, managers and their guests on your invitation list. The better the standing the firm has in the community the more credibility your exhibition will have. Do your research and make your approach, this will be one of the times when the flexibility of your dates will be important. Around September next year allows the recipient of your request a little leeway. If dates are specified the opportunities are being restricted. There may be something vital happening on that particular day, but a week later may be ideal. The company may want to help, but tied to a specific date may find themselves unable to cooperate.

There will, for the same reasons, need to be flexibility with regard to the duration of your needs. Whilst one day and evening for a private view may be easy to accommodate, for those of you wishing to use the venue for the whole exhibition the availability will help to determine the length of time for which the exhibition is to run.

If you decide on this route, again write and confirm the arrangements you have come to, and again be reliable. The firm may have their own P.R. department, work closely with them to ensure that the firm and your exhibition obtain maximum press coverage, after all this will be one of their main reasons for hosting the event. If the project works successfully for both parties it could well become an annual event.

You may have a client who would willingly allow you to use part of their premises. The venue could be as diverse as a reception area in the town or a large house in the country in its own grounds. The use of private premises would be unusual and a rare privilege not to be abused.

Colleges or other public buildings are also good venues for exhibitions. The research and the approach will be the same as that of the firms and hotels but with local government or college bureaucracy. Red tape being the way it is, it may take you longer to ascertain who is in a position to authorise the venture. A good ally on this occasion would be your local councillor. He/she may be able to put you in touch with the right person and may also be able to put in a good word for you. Here again, there may be an existing guest list for the private view, although probably not as commercial as one would like. There may also be organisers and P.R. staff for you to work with. You could be very lucky in that they may take the whole show on board, right down to the financing, advertising, etc. Don't get complacent though, as with the gallery, work with these people to ensure the best possible chance of success.

Obviously, to hold an exhibition at your own premises would be ideal. One is able to continue working if things are quiet or to be the genial host if they are not. It can be soul-destroying to man an exhibition when it is quiet, trying very hard to look busy and attentive all the time for when clients do come in. Your own premises may be big enough for the follow-on days of the exhibition when you are expecting a trickle of one or two visitors at any one time, but not big enough for the private view.

It is possible to hold a successful exhibition with the private view at one venue and the general exhibition at your own premises. It is easier and less expensive to hire a large room for a day and an evening for the private view than for one or two weeks for the whole event. Most of your invited guests already know you and where you are based and visitors to the general exhibition will be coming to your own showroom. This has the added advantage that these people will know where to find you in future.

Another venue is a shop or chain store. If you choose wisely, and your approach and proposition is sound, as with the company, you will find willing hosts. Here again you will be able to add to your guest list, and an added bonus of 'passing trade'.

The venue I'm saving till last, either because it may be totally unsuitable or because it will need a great deal of work to make it acceptable is the local village church or community halls. One immediately thinks of trestle tables lined with jam pots, but this need not necessarily be true. You should not dismiss the hall out of hand. Go and look objectively at it; some halls are lovely with a charm all of their own and others are totally unsuitable. If it is unsuitable, don't compromise, reject it.

There are, as you will now know, many possibilities both within and outside your range. Get yourself organised, settle down and work out which is best for you.

Leave nothing to chance. When you find your venue, book it and set the time. As you can now see from all the different factors that govern the various feasible venues, the duration of the exhibition will almost be decided for you, either by the people you will need to work with, or by finances. The space you have chosen will also dictate whether or not a review of the number of exhibits involved will be needed.

Now a venue, a date, and a time span, joint or sole exhibition and number of pieces have been established. You are well and truly on the rails, and have started a demanding journey.

This is the time to confirm details to other makers who are to join the venture. You will have been unable to give them specific details until now. You will only have ascertained their interest in the venture until this point, but now you have something concrete to offer and should therefore obtain firm agreements and deposits from them at this stage.

Several makers taking part in the exhibition will obviously spread the burden of the expenses and will make the actual cost of the exhibition easier to bear. Be very clear in your initial discussions with your colleagues how costs are to be met, so that you do not end up with all the bills, chasing everyone for payment. The ideal is for all to contribute an equal amount of money to a fund based on your anticipated costs of the exhibition and a contingency allowance. This should be banked separately and good clear accounts kept. It is much simpler to redistribute an overpayment than to collect a deficiency. The contract may or may not allow for a share out of surplus funds at the end, should there be any.

Perhaps this is now the ideal time to discuss how you are financing the venture. If you have a private income then you may not be concerned about this aspect, but not many are in that position and therefore the finances are important.

You may feel that the time scale is such that you can realistically do commissions whilst preparing for the exhibition and keep your head above water. You may continue to sell your work and collect it back for the exhibition. But for those of you who have decided that everything is going to be for sale and the lead time is only enough for exhibition preparation then there are really only two options. You will either need a bank loan or you will need to find someone else to pay, eg.sponsorship or a grant, (see Chapter 8).

Personally, I don't like the idea of sponsorship and grants, the phrase 'easy come – easy go' springs readily to mind and if it's not your money and your commitment then I feel one's effort will not be one hundred percent. There are also parameters to which you may be restricted, but it is a personal decision. You will also have to take on board the idea that you may have to defend your need to be sponsored or aided and you may not wish to do that.

A rudimentary information sheet is the next step. It should be written out on your headed notepaper, setting out the basic details of your exhibition but omitting the details of the private view. This should then be printed out. With the cost of instant print services it should be quite an economical operation. All participants of a joint exhibition should receive their own supply of these information sheets. Of course if there are several exhibitors it may not be appropriate to use your own notepaper, but perhaps a logo or heading designed specifically for the exhibition. In this way you can explain to potential and existing clients, as you meet them in the course of the work, about the exhibition. Enthuse quietly, if that's not too much of a contradiction. Tell them what a super opportunity it will be to see so much of your work together, the full range of your abilities, etc. You will then be able to give them the information sheet to take away and make a note of the dates, being careful to explain to them that the private view will be the evening or the day before and that they will of course receive an invitation nearer the time.

Some people may warrant just a general 'Do come along, we'd be very pleased to see you, here's a note of the dates and venue.' This is why preview details are left off the general information sheet.

It is easy to invite everyone and I will never forget my first exhibition preview. Being a complete novice I had invited everybody I could think of whether or not they were potential buyers. I spent more time and nervous energy watching two would-be drunks demolishing the wine stocks than I did attending to clients. You will find for very little cost this information sheet will do its work until you start in earnest at the printers.

If you are to employ road signs from one of the automobile associations, it is a good idea to process the request early as they will need to get local authority permission. It can be a good idea to ask them where they intend to place the signs to ensure that all the routes to the venue are covered.

Insurance cover must be carefully thought about. Your own existing business policy may be valid for public liability away from your premises but there will probably be an extra premium to pay to insure the work away from your own premises on exhibition. Read carefully through the part of your policy relating to transportation to ensure that you are fully covered in that respect. Some venues will require that you insure against damage to their property.

Six months before the exhibition you must begin work on your press releases and contacting the media (see Chapter 14). Remember that some of the magazines, television and radio programmes have long lead times. Do not be inflexible in your dealings, if one of the journalists you approach wants to do a feature two months before the exhibition, it would be foolish to refuse, expecting them to return when it suited you.

This is also the time to consider advertising the event in the local glossy magazines and the local press (see Chapter 14). This can be very expensive and only you can decide whether or not to do it. If you use a photograph it would be a good idea to use the same one as you are going to use on your literature, even if the advert is to be black and white, the image will be the same. Remember two or three lines on the 'What's on' page could be just as useful and it will be free, though the entry cannot be guaranteed.

At least three months before the exhibition talk to your printer (see Chapter 11) to ascertain how much lead time he will need for the advance publicity, posters, catalogues, price lists and invitations. This will ensure that everything is ready on time and nothing is rushed. It is important that all the literature hangs together. For example, the colour and typeface should be the same; the photograph on the postcard should be the same as the one on the poster and the front of the catalogue. Not only does this look good, but it also helps to reinforce a positive image in a similar way to advertising on the television.

Advance publicity should begin to circulate about one month before the exhibition. Postcards are suitable for this purpose and you may find some of the firms advertised in trade magazines will be competitive on price but variable on quality. A postcard is small, will tuck into a pocket, handbag or diary. Many of the venues you approach to display them will find the size acceptable. You can get a tempting photograph on the front and all the information you need on to the back. They can be distributed in a number of ways. By the participants, who will now replace the previous advance publicity leaflet with the new postcards and at strategic local gathering places. Restrict yourself to a radius of so many miles around the venue and to the places prospective clients are likely to frequent. Within this radius there will be good hotels, restaurants, hairdressers, etc. which may be prepared to carry them for you. Good hotels like to advise their guests what is going on in the vicinity and look upon it as part of the service they offer. Other venues have differing attitudes, sometimes one can elicit a favourable response by visiting personally. When deciding how many cards to have printed allow for the number of participants and the number of venues you can expect to leave them with. You will find that ten in each place is about average.

With the advances in photocopying, full-coloured posters are no longer prohibitively expensive. The size you have printed will depend on where you intend to place them. A4, while not being huge and eye catching, will be much more acceptable and you will therefore be able to place more of them. Again, fix a radius and place them where your prospective clients are most likely to see them. These should be in place about one week before the event.

It would be a courtesy, if it is appropriate, to give an invitation to the private view to owners of private hotels, restaurants, etc. who are willing to assist you by displaying your advance publicity. It may even result in a new client.

There are different schools of thought about when invitations should be sent. One is that you must send the invitation about a month before the event to allow your client to put it in the diary before the date becomes booked up. The other is that if you send it too early it will be forgotten and nearer the date it will be more immediate. Personally, I favour sending the invitations early, three or four weeks before the exhibition. Then there is yet another set of thinking about day of the week on which the invitation should be received to attract most attention. Saturday seems to be the most favoured day, when it is reputed that busy people have more time to look through their personal post. With the vagaries of the post one certainly could not predict the delivery day of the mail using second class post. However, if you use first class post, the Post Office does guarantee a high percentage of next day delivery. Care should be taken to strike the right note with the invitation. It should not look like a wedding invitation, yet it should be special and inviting, something that your client will want to place on the mantelpiece or wherever else important invitations are kept. (see Chapter 11). The envelope containing the invitation should be of good quality paper and the address written in a good hand. If your handwriting is not up to this task and you are unable to inveigle a colleague with a good hand to do it for you then the envelopes must be typed. Do not use sticky computer labels. You are not sending out some tacky circular, but the invitation to your exhibition. It is important, treat it as such. The aim is to make the invitation stand out like a beacon in a plethora of ordinary mail.

Sending a catalogue with the invitation is an excellent way of providing a small preview of your exhibition to your clients, further encouraging them to come along to the private view. For the clients unable to attend it will serve to keep them abreast with what you are doing. They may, if they are familiar with your work, have the confidence to buy from the catalogue. Your catalogues will be scattered far and wide in the right places – your clients' homes, where they will be passed around and shown or given away to friends, leaving some clients asking for replacements. They can cover the whole gamut of what will be on offer or just a few pieces as a sample. Catalogues that contain only a few of the items on offer can be accompanied by the price list which will of course list everything with descriptions and prices. In this way the client will be advised that the pieces in the catalogue are not all that is available, although this should be clearly stated in the catalogue.

The price list is of course vital. If you do not have a catalogue printed then it will not be very subtle to send the price list on its own with the invitation. They should be available at the private view beside the visitors book for your guest to collect as they enter. A good size for a price list is A5. Depending on the size of the exhibition they can be a small booklet or a single card. This will be easy for your client to handle, along with the glass of wine.

A month or two before the exhibition you will have to decide how many workers you will need to employ for the private view. I use the word 'employ' in the loosest possible way because you may have reliable friends and relatives that you can call upon, who will be only too happy to be involved and to help. Be sure to show your appreciation in whatever form will be most acceptable. Sometimes however, you may have to properly employ someone and that should be budgeted for.

At the private view you must be free to talk to clients. There must be someone to greet the guests and ask them to sign the visitors book, show them where the wine is, point out where you are, hand them a catalogue or price list and be genuinely pleased to see them. There must be someone at hand to attend to the drinks, keeping a selection of wine, orange juice and water readily to hand, and clearing away used glasses. A presence at the drinks table stops people taking advantage of your generosity and that is very important. If you are chatting to a prospective client and want to refill his glass, that will then be your choice.

Then there must be someone apart from yourself who knows about your work so that if you are tied up there is not a client waiting, getting fed up with waiting, losing interest and going away. It is very important to treat all your clients and prospective clients as if they were special; they are special, without them you cannot pursue your chosen occupation. They must not feel neglected so do try to ensure that you find time for everyone and that someone familiar with your work is also on hand to ensure that all your guests are informatively spoken to. Some of your visitors may have travelled a good distance, if they are ignored it will kill the sale and discourage the visitor from attending again. A private view should be a special occasion and your guests will arrive full of expectation and good wishes; having worked so hard to arrive at this moment, don't spoil it.

You must decide if you need anyone outside to help with the car parking and directing people to the venue. Also if you need assistance on setting-up day.

The setting up is something that must be going through your mind as you work towards your exhibition. How to display the work to best advantage. With the choice of venue the parameters for the problem have been set and you will have to work within that framework. As with your literature, work to make everything hang together. The colour of the plinths and drapes should blend or contrast with the surroundings and enhance the pieces. The more attention you pay to details such as this the more impressed your visitors will be. (See Chapter5).

The area by the door is equally as important as the exhibition itself. Here is where clients will be greeted, asked to sign the visitors book, offered a drink, given a price list and perhaps later on sign a cheque. Allow plenty of room for these activities. The tables you use should be clean and uncluttered covered with a suitable cloth if appropriate. The visitors book (do not forget a ample supply of reasonable pens) and catalogues/price lists should be prominently placed, along with a no smoking sign for the comfort of all of your guests. If you are a smoker you should not ignore your own request, neither should you keep rushing out, neglecting your visitors, to smoke. Drinks should be served from another table. It cannot be stressed enough how important this area is, it will be here that the first impression is formed, there should be no half-eaten sandwiches or dirty glasses in evidence.

It is always beneficial while contemplating the setting up of the exhibition to compile a list of things needed either for setting up, for display or required for the private view. This will ensure that you have everything you might need and are able to work to maximum efficiency.

When you are happy with your layout and greeting point, make sure the floor is clean, then go around carefully and dust everything, touch up plinths and make sure no raw edges are showing on the fabric drapes. Finally put in place the numbers to coincide with the price list.

When all is ready place some of the wine glasses on the table ensuring that fresh ones are to hand but not visible. Check that the white wine, fruit juice and mineral water are in the fridge and that the red wine is at room temperature. This selection of drinks is an ideal compromise and whilst it would be very nice to offer red or white wine, dry, medium or sweet; orange, pineapple or grapefruit juice; still or aerated water, it would take far too long. Wine merchants are usually very good at suggesting acceptable wines within your price range. It is also possible to buy the wine on sale or return to ensure that you do not run out. Glasses are usually loaned free, and sometimes not only will the merchant deliver the wine, but they will have started the cooling procedure for you. Local small merchants, even though they might be part of a big chain, can be appreciative of your business and therefore most helpful. Depending on the prestige of the event, the expected numbers of guests and the budget involved, you may feel it appropriate to serve champagne. The glasses usually loaned by the wine merchant can sometimes be quite a motley selection, and again depending on the calibre of the event you may feel that it would be prudent to purchase your own glasses. It is possible now to get acceptable imported crystal very reasonably priced in the quantities you will need.

None of us feel we need lessons on appearance. However, it would be very foolish having spent all the time, money and effort on your work, the organisation, the printing, the setting up, etc. and denying yourself that last little bit of confidence. Dress for the occasion. You and your work are the centre of attention; do not let yourself down. This is a very special occasion, you have done everything you can to ensure that the whole experience is special. Your clients will be 'captured' by the moment, by the ambience and general feeling of being somewhere special where 'things' are really happening. A significant step for one of tomorrow's acclaimed craftsmen – don't spoil it by appearing in old jeans and a sweater.

Now you have to stop worrying. There is nothing more you can do, everything is in place. Friends, family or employees have their designated jobs. Enjoy the moment, be the genial host, attend to your guest with confidence. Do not indulge in your own hospitality until it is all over and the last guest has left.

Don't be shy about money. That is what it is all about. You and your helpers must be alert and sensitive to people who want to make a purchase or place a commission. Do not push a sale, be receptive and helpful. A red spot placed on the identification number of the exhibit is the accepted way of denoting that the piece is sold. Whilst you may place a red spot with confidence for an established customer without the immediate transfer of funds, it would be foolhardy to extend this trust to an unfamiliar client. It effectively takes the piece off the market. If the sale were subsequently to fall through for any reason you have lost your most advantageous selling time.

It would of course be wonderful if all of the monies owed were paid there and then, but it is not always feasible. Clients who know you very well, may simply interrupt a conversation you are having long enough to say 'We are leaving now. Thank you for inviting us. We have decided to have number twelve. I will telephone you in the week.' You cannot possibly extricate yourself from what could be an important conversation other than to say 'Of course. I will attend to it. Goodbye. Thank you for coming.' Neither could you contemplate running after him to ask for payment. Some clients will give you deposits, or pay in full. Others will expect to pay when the piece is collected or delivered.

Give your helpers firm guidelines about sales. They should be seen to be decisive and helpful, even if their role is simply to bring the client to you to secure the sale. It would be unfair, for them to be expected to make the same personal judgements that you may make about whether or not a red spot should be placed without at least a deposit.

Always take money with good grace, with a flourish even. Talk about the piece, how much you have enjoyed making it and where the idea came from. Show the purchaser where it is signed and particular features you are pleased with. They are spending a lot of money – reinforce their choice of piece – if appropriate ask where it will be placed in their home. They have paid you the ultimate in compliments. Not only do they like your work, but they are prepared to part with their hard earned cash to own it, and finally they like it enough to want to look at it everyday. Always ensure red dots go on the pieces immediately so that there are no mix-ups.

You will, during the balance of your exhibition time, realise that all your work leading up to the exhibition was mainly for the few hours of your private view. It has been my experience that there will not be the same sales potential through the rest of the time the work is exhibited. The odd new customer may come forward and the odd invited guest who was unable to attend the private view but generally sales will be quieter. Nevertheless, the exhibition must stay tidy, well dusted with an attentive attendant. During this quieter time you should contact all your purchasers and make arrangements for delivery and collection of their chosen pieces.

When the exhibition is over there will be no time to rest, follow up every commission and every lead. Transfer names and addresses of new and prospective clients on to your indexes. You may also have some new entries for the information only file. Take care when you are sifting through the names and addresses in your visitors book of general visitors to the exhibition. I have always found it useful to discreetly mark entries in the visitors book as memory aids as to which index, if any, they should be added. All the sold pieces must be packed and then delivered to, or collected by, their various owners. This will be when the last of the accounts are usually settled. When the dust has settled critically review the exhibition, analyse how successful it was, identify areas that worked very well and what improvements you feel could be made next time. Learn from the experience.

It is possible to employ exhibition organisers to do all this work for a fee. As with all other unknown quantities the research will be vital. Find out what you are getting for your money, the quality and success of previous events, etc. Remember, the organiser will expect to be paid regardless of the profitability and sales generated.

CHAPTER FOURTEEN

The Media

To become an established craftsman with a reputation, not only do you have to produce quality products of good design, package, promote and market your work, but you have to maintain a constant image in the public eye and more particularly with your current and prospective clients. This will gradually instil in them a confidence that will reinforce their will to purchase work from you. Like a constant but gentle dripping of water on stone – gradually it makes an impression on the hardest of surfaces. So to go along with your new found skills you must also add that of maintaining a profile through the media.

It is not beyond the bounds of possibility that one article will result in a direct sale, but this is unusual and not to be expected as the norm. What we are working towards is the positive reinforcement of your position with your existing clients and encouraging new ones – creating, with the help of the media, your promotional skills, exhibitions, etc. the ideal situations that enhance reputations – building the knock-on effect, so that if someone sees your work in the media, in the home of an acquaintance, at an exhibition or elsewhere, a bell will ring and they will say to themselves 'Is this not the craftsman/artist Fred Bloggs in the paper, magazine, on the radio or television? We saw his work at such and such an exhibition? Wasn't it Mr and Mrs Smith who were saying a few weeks ago that they had had something made by him? Don't you remember them saying how pleased they were with the piece and the service they received?' – This is what reputations and good client lists are made of. This is the profile we are aiming for. All of these new skills are tools, you must learn how to use them, but never rely on any particular one alone.

The media can help, although it can be very expensive if you are going to place advertising, but one small editorial feature can be worth several large advertisements. Editorial is seen as unsolicited praise, whereas advertising is recognised as purchased space.

In order for the media to give you some editorial space you have to provide them with an item of interest for their readers, initially in the form of a press release. Articles are generally written by their own staff or commissioned from a free-lance journalist. So here we will only deal with press releases and interviews.

The great trick with a press release is to get your item out of the envelope and onto the editorial desk, rather than out of the envelope and into the rubbish bin. I was once told, but have never checked the veracity of the information, that at one of the national newspaper offices the rubbish bin for unused press releases consists of an oil drum which is filled daily. We have to get past this oil drum.

I have read many books and talked to many 'experts' on this subject and there are no hard and fast rules as to how to get your press release accepted and published. There are, however, many things that you can do to stack the cards in your favour as it were, but when you have done all you can there is still an element of fingers crossed and here we go, as you place your mailing in the post box. A small glimmer of hope that you can cling to is that all media channels: newspapers, magazines, radio and television have to fill their pages and programmes every day, every week and every month. Someone has to be featured – why not you? If you can get the right idea to the right person – why not indeed?

The general rules for approaching the media are the same for all branches, local, national and international; radio, television, newspapers and magazines, the only difference will be the lead time required. That is the time needed by the editorial/research department from the receipt of the information (press release) to the time the newspapers and magazines go to press. If you are working to a deadline, for example an exhibition or an award, then you must work backwards from when the item will be taking place and ensure that you allow plenty of time. Some magazines work with a three month lead time; that is to say a piece to go in the September issue must be received by June. Sometimes this does seem a little early, but if you are planning an exhibition in September then of course you know long before June and it is not onerous to ensure that the magazines that require this amount of lead time get the press releases in time. One thing that may confuse you somewhat is that some magazines issue their September Issue in August and a three month lead time for this issue will therefore be May. But beware if you wish the promotional piece for an exhibition to appear in September rather than the September issue (out in August), then you must plan accordingly. Don't forget to take into account the date of issue, 1st September means before 1st of June and so on. You will get the hang of things. The directories mentioned later give lead times and deadlines.

The other timing device available to you is the embargo. This is the date before which you do not wish the information to be released. In the field of arts and crafts this would rarely be used, but it is useful for prize-givings and items such as that. It is not a good idea for the winners, or losers for that matter, to discover the results through the media before the occasion. The embargo date should be written clearly at the top of the page with the word EMBARGO written boldly beside it.

You must define your audience and target the media channel that is appropriate. It would be a waste of time, effort and energy to send a press release about leather handbags to 'Angler's Weekly'. Not only is the item unlikely to be run, but in the unlikely event that it was run it would be of little interest to fishermen discussing ways and means of catching fish. Likewise makers of more expensive items must circulate the media that cater for the more affluent members of society. Target only the channels you feel your clients will read, hear or watch.

The value of having items run in your own trade press is a debatable one, but one that over the years I have learned not to scorn. Whilst it must be accepted that the majority of readers will be doers and not buyers, it does not mean that there are no clients and potential clients within this group. Good quality articles in your own trade magazines can enhance your reputation amongst your peers, and give you valuable experience at preparing press releases and articles and giving interviews. It is good for the ego when you begin to do this work for yourself to actually score a hit, and it is much more probable that your own specialist trade magazine will run an item about an exponent of its own specialisation.

Local media exists on local stories, and generally the local newspapers are read across the social strata by those who are interested in the local news. The local free sheets are not such a good idea, because they are not seen as serious newspapers and therefore, your item will assume by association the trivia perceived. The item must however have a local flavour, about people, places and/or events within their own circulation area; exhibitions, national awards or a special commission for a local resident, for example.

The item will benefit from being current and topical. A friend of mine grew roses before he retired and when Prince Andrew married Sarah Ferguson he was asked to supply some of the roses for the occasion. A local free-lance journalist was able to place this topical story with a local glossy magazine and the result was a four page colour article. Many cabinet makers and other craftsmen in wood were able to capitalise on the hurricane of 1987 not only for their timber, but for their publicity. Everyone was interested in knowing what happened to all the magnificent trees that were so unceremoniously uprooted, and were pleased to be reassured that beautiful things had been made with the wood and that all was not lost. Items about hurricane trees were current and topical for at least a year after the storm and were frequently run in all forms of media, both local and national. Heaven forfend that we should all start praying for another small disaster to increase the 'publishability' of press releases and articles in our own particular field, but I'm sure that this illustrates the point very well.

The media cannot be seen to be giving away free advertising space to a commercial business, no matter how small it may appear. The fee paying advertisers would, justifiably, be aggrieved. To this end the news item must always have a strong element of human interest and not be seen to overtly advertise your products. With the client's permission, a significant commission may be of interest, or your acceptance as artist in residence at a local school, your making of a community project from local materials, an exhibition will be of interest for the arts page. The presentation of a national award, taking part in an international exhibition, making the biggest, the smallest, the tallest or the longest. Look all the time for the necessary 'angles' on what you are doing – artists/craftsmen have the human interest built in, if only they could tap into it. You must get into the habit of thinking through what you are doing and teasing away at whether or not it is newsworthy, topical or could contain an element of human interest. With practice you will learn to recognise the occasions when it is worth the effort of writing a press release and sending it off.

Whenever possible send your press release in an envelope addressed to an individual, rather than to the editorial office, or diary dates, or to the art editor. I'm not saying that it will not achieve its aim sent otherwise, but it does perhaps stand a better chance going to a specific target than a more general one.

There are many ways of establishing to whom you send your releases. If you are unsure of the names and styles of some of the newspapers and magazines go either to your local reference library or to one of the big newsagents, where they will not frown upon a browser, and study them. You may prefer to buy a few at a time and study them at home at your leisure. Not only will this help you with your placement of the press releases, but it will help with your targeting of particular newspapers and magazines. When you see an article or news item that could just as easily have been about you or your field and it is in a magazine or newspaper that you feel would be beneficial note down the author of the article, and the name and address of the magazine. The author's name should be with the article, if not, perhaps in the list of contents and features at the front. The address of the magazine is usually to be found at the front, if it proves to be a more difficult one to find, it can usually be located on the 'Letters to the Editor' page. This name and address should be added to your press file. Sometimes using this method can prove more beneficial than using the large media directories because it is possible that the author, whom you have noted down, is in fact a free-lance and therefore not on the staff of the magazine. Had you sent your item to the magazine staff direct it may never come to the attention of this particular free-lance who (if you have chosen well) may be sympathetic to your cause and therefore more interested in what you are doing.

This method can also be used for radio and television. The name you want may be found at the end of the programme entry in the television and radio journals, or when the titles are read or shown in the programme credits, the researchers will be listed. Whilst it may seem a good idea to send your item to the presenter, it is the people behind the scenes who put the programmes together, and usually the researchers who compile the initial material.

There are large and expensive media directories and they should be available in all good reference libraries. The one I am most familiar with is 'The P.R. Planner; it claims to list all publications, television and radio programmes. It is divided into specialisations of national publications, areas of local publications, television and radio. Under each separate heading for individual publications and programmes it lists the editors and contacts for special interests. It also advises the lead times necessary and the interests of the readers or audience. The necessary updates to these publications are also expensive, prolific and usually produced on a monthly basis, if you use a library copy ensure that the updates are current. You will be unable to rely on the information if it is not kept up to date.

Finally, if all else fails, receptionists can sometimes be very helpful if you are unsure as to whom you should send your press release. Telephone the newspaper, magazine, television or radio station in question and ask politely, explain broadly the area of interest, and if he is unsure he will be able to put you in touch with someone that will know.

Local (and not so local) free-lance journalists can also be very good contacts. They earn their living by writing and placing articles and photographs in the media, and it is in their interests therefore, to get an item placed. Some of them serve radio and television as well as the press and they have contacts in both local and national media. Their names are generally listed in the local directories, (Yellow Pages, for example) some with their areas of interests, some not, which is a little disconcerting as you may well send your press release to a racing correspondent if you do not check their field first. Telephone them and ask what subjects they cover. As long as you are polite and considerate with the timing of your call I'm sure it will be well received, after all you may be potential business. Having said this, and theoretically the principle still holds good, during the recession of the early 1990's the media were cutting back on costs as much as everyone else and were therefore reluctant to pay a free-lance journalist when through direct press releases and judicious use of their own staff they could produce their own items. Judge the climate for yourself at the time; you will probably find that the free-lance journalist will tell you if you have more chance with a direct press release.

Now to the press release. It must be contained if at all possible on one sheet of A4. It must have wide margins and double line spacing, this will facilitate the reading of the piece and editing for use. It must be remembered at every stage that we are doing all we can to make it as easy as possible to edit and use the press release. The words PRESS RELEASE should be printed boldly at the top of the page, this advises journalists that it is potential incoming copy and should not be confused with letters or advertising. Next your logo, if you have one. Then the address and contact telephone number, both daytime and evening, (media staff work unusual hours) with the name of either yourself or someone competent to deal with the media on your behalf, followed by the embargo if used. A short heading is next, and try as you might you will be unable to excel the journalese and pure 'corn' of the headline writers. Make sure that the subject of the press release is contained in the heading. Always remember you are trying to catch and hold the attention of the person whose job it is to sift through the press releases.

Next the text. It must answer the who, what, where, when and perhaps the how and why questions. The sentences should be shorter than normal, as should the paragraphs. The information succinctly and simply delivered with impact. Ensure the piece is easy to read, all the information is present, and that you have not rambled on in a confused manner (or in any manner). At the end put 'The End', so that it is clear there are no more pages to the press release. After which you should put the date, in order to indicate when the item is no longer current. At which end you put the date is immaterial, as long as it cannot be confused with the embargo.

It all sounds so simple! But it can be very difficult to write positively and flatteringly about oneself or one's work. For the same reasons I mentioned earlier when discussing brochures (Chapter 11), never use the first person. It is a sound idea to accompany a press release with a good clear photograph. All types of photographs can now be processed by the media, some of course still have their preferences, and depending on what type of printing they are using some will work better than others. Therefore, I still advocate colour slides for colour work and glossy prints for black and white work. The photograph is one way to attract attention as your press release travels from the envelope to the rubbish bin. A good, clear, informative, attractive picture will encourage the closer reading of your press release, and action upon it. If you are sending a slide it is perhaps wise to enclose a reproduction of the slide to encourage a closer look. If you are reluctant to send a slide, send only the reproduction, a good, bright, glossy colour photograph and add at the base of your press release and the caption of the photograph 'Slides are available immediately' (of course you will ensure that they are).

The picture must be able to stand on its own and to tell a story with only the aid of the small caption that you attach to it. This will give you in effect 'two bites at the cherry', the first is the opportunity for the magazine to use the press release and the photograph in a small item, the second being for them to fill a space with just the photograph and the caption. Therefore, put some thought into the content of the photograph. The lectern commissioned by the local church will look much better with the vicar reading from it, or better still, re-adjusted with the vicar's pretty 10 year old daughter reading from it. And you have the benefit of adding the human interest. Try not to make the photograph staid or impersonal, look at it critically and ask yourself what story is it telling.

A caption must be attached to the photograph with cellotape so that it hangs down below the photograph, but folds up behind it, or it can be on one of the sticky labels that you can buy on rolls in many sizes. Do not write directly on the back of the photograph in either pencil, pen or any other fancy marker. If the lettering does not indent the front of the photograph it is sure to smudge or run. The caption should be typed and contain the basic information necessary to identify the picture and its contents. It may unwittingly get separated from the press release, so it needs enough information to be reunited or to stand on its own.

Who takes your photographs is up to you, this aspect is discussed in Chapter 11, but I would re-iterate that if you go to a photographer that he is not solely a wedding photographer used to outdoor colour work of people. You will be, by the nature of your profession, probably photographing a three dimensional object with or without people with appropriate surroundings. For any publication it must be right. Do not be afraid to ask the photographer if he is able to undertake the work, or to 'discuss' the account if the work is not up to scratch.

It is debatable whether or not there is any value in sending your C.V. with the press release, just as with whether or not one should send a slide rather than simply the reproduction. You can note on your press release that a colour slide and C.V. is immediately available, allowing for the journalist to get in touch if interested. This will save you money on the cost of the mailing. The obverse of this argument is that if you present all the ingredients necessary to make a small article, the journalist can get on with the item, no messing about with phone calls and waiting for the paperwork to be delivered and perhaps a more imminent deadline will be met with your piece. It is a debate with two sides and only you can decide which way you want to work.

There are also two schools of thought on the follow up. On the one hand it is suggested that you telephone each of the press release recipients to ensure that your item has been received, whether or not it will be covered and if more information is required. Personally, I do not find this very useful. If you have done your homework properly, unless the Post Office and internal mail distribution services have broken down, then of course your piece has been delivered. If it has been properly presented then hopefully it has been noticed. Whether or not they cover it will be their decision qualified each step of the way by the many influences that come into play as a publication deadline approaches. If they require any further information, they have your address and telephone number and will be in touch. Journalists, by the nature of their jobs, are busy people with deadlines to meet and if everyone who sent them a press release rang them the switchboard would be in chaos. I choose to do my homework and research thoroughly and cross my fingers. It may not be scientific, but neither is running up your telephone account – the results will be the same.

Many firms and businesses hire agencies to do this work and to mail the media. Agencies will have established contacts with the media. They will have a flair for knowing what can be made newsworthy and how to do it and, an enviable ability to write press releases and choose the appropriate photographs. They are expensive and charge for effort rather than results, which can be as hit and miss as your own, although probably more hit than yours while you are learning and finding your feet. I'm not convinced of their value for artists and craftsmen, but it is perhaps a spiral – when at last you can afford them, do you employ them because you can afford them, rather than because you need them, or do you employ them to take one of your many peripheral duties off your hands, leaving you more time in the workshop and studio? When and if you do get to employ an agency do your homework and ensure that you are getting what you are paying for which will probably be the experience of an established employer rather than the new office boy. The credentials for P.R. work are still in their infancy – it is a whole new service industry.

This may all seem a bit too much like hard work, and more than a bit hit and miss, but once you are 'programmed into Press Release Mode' you will be surprised at how your mind will quietly work away, only to spring to attention when you are doing something that can be made into a newsworthy item. The plus factor that you must always remember is that newspaper and magazine pages, television and radio programmes have to be filled day after day, week after week, month after month, year after year and really if the truth be known, you are helping them to fill space!

The reward when you see your first piece in the media is tremendous – not necessarily in immediate sales but as a boost to your ego and confidence that having done it once you can do it again; helping to instil amongst both present and future clients confidence and reassurance in you, your work and their decision to patronise you.

If however the media do not use your press release verbatim, or do not extract pieces to use, but telephone you for further information – do not be thrown off your guard. Do not, unless you are experienced in these matters accept an interview, no matter how brief, there and then. It is easy enough if someone else answers the telephone on your behalf for them to say that you are busy and that you will return the call as soon as possible. If you answer your own telephone to a journalist, explain that you are with a client and that you will return the call. It goes without saying that either you or your assistant will take proper details, ie, name of journalist, name of the organization represented, telephone number and convenient time to return the call. It may seem obvious, but when you are new to this aspect of your trade, the euphoria of having scored a hit may send trivial things like asking for details right out of your head. Use this time to compose yourself, even if it is only ten minutes, it will be most helpful in collecting your thoughts and giving a successful interview. Make a quick note of answers to questions that may arise from the press release and have it beside you when you return the call so that, from sheer nervousness, you do not contradict yourself and you are able to be accurate about dates, spellings, etc.

When you then talk to the journalist, be confident – but not cocky, self-assured – but not boastful. Telephone interviews can be so easily distorted, and if you are not careful you can be portrayed in a very bad light. Keep things simple, do not go into long and involved explanations. If the interviewer had wanted an in-depth longer piece an appointment would be made for a proper interview.

Sometimes the journalist will make an appointment to come to your work-shop for an interview and possibly some photographs. These meetings usually take longer than predicted and are more relaxed than anticipated. In most craftsman/artist situations the interview is not expected to be contentious and the journalist will not be seeking to ensnare you into lively debate. Nevertheless they make seek information that you are not prepared to part with, for example names of clients or costs of commissions, etc. Prices may be public knowledge, as with exhibition catalogues, priced work, or a public authority commission, on the other hand it may not and you must be prepared to be firm and protect the anonymity of your client and the depth to which he has dug into his pocket.

Television and radio interviews are much more harrowing experiences than those for newspapers and magazines. Some are recorded for later use and others are live. Here, as before, you need composure time. You may be tempted, either at home or in the hospitality room before the interview at the studio, to have a little something to steady your nerves. Don't do it! Nothing stronger than coffee must pass your lips, you may relax and be indiscreet and say something that you will not be able to retract.

It is a good idea, when your appointment is made for the interview, to ask what you are likely to be asked so that you can do some preparatory work, although chances are that the interviewer will have only a general idea rather than a firm line of questions. Ensure that you take with you the press release that instigated the interview, and any other relevant information that you may forget at just the wrong moment. Remember, it is possible to forget your mother's birthday when you have an audience! As long as you go prepared in this most rudimentary manner, you can afford to relax a little; the subject of the interview is one that you know back to front and inside out – you and your work.

I have recently read an article advising craftsmen/artists how to deal with the media, and it suggested that one should not change clothes for an interview. I am assuming that this refers to the photography session, and I am not sure what the thinking is behind this. I would suggest that it is better to be clean and tidy when being interviewed and photographed, or recorded on film for the television, thereby projecting an air of professionalism, rather than to appear in one's working clothes, giving an impression of 'so what?' 'who cares?'. I am obviously not suggesting one's best ballgown, or a suit and tie, but the right note can and must be struck.

If the request for an interview comes out of the blue, then it is even more important that you discover why they want to interview you, on what subject and what form the questions are likely to take. Never forget that the media serves its own interests before it serves your's and they may be wanting your opinion on something that, whilst you may feel quite strongly about, you do not wish your opinions to be made public as it may alienate you from some of your clients. For instance, if during parliamentary elections, the Labour Party make a pledge to place an artist/craftsman in residence in every senior school in the country, your opinion may be sought. I am not saying that such an opinion should not be given. What I am saying is, be careful that if you do agree to be interviewed on this topic that you do not say anything that will alienate either your Conservative, Labour or S.D.P. clients. There are many ways to express one particular point of view and if you want to take part in the interview ensure that you go very well prepared and are not pushed into saying something that you will have plenty of time to regret. And do not be afraid to decline the interview if that is what you would prefer. On the other hand they may have been storing past press releases with the intention of interviewing you one day and today's the day. It does no harm to ask and you will be better prepared.

It is normal practice for you to meet the interviewer before the interview takes place. This is generally informal, and takes the form of a quick chat to clarify points on which the interviewer is unclear. The importance of this meeting should never be underestimated. It serves the purpose of you meeting each other in a relaxed atmosphere and ensuring that you know where you will be going, what will happen and answering any queries you may have, etc. This will be far more important with a live television interview than with a recorded one. It is unlikely that any interviewer will be familiar with technicalities of your art/craft and the other purpose of the meeting will be to run through what you do and how you do it so that they do not make any real blunders on air. The interviewer will also at this time have a much clearer idea of what questions you will be asked and may even ask you if there are any particular points that have been obviously neglected and which you would wish to mention.

I personally know of live interview experience which has turned out to be very difficult because of a lack of understanding by the interviewer who had not bothered to meet those being interviewed prior to the broadcast. It is therefore wise to insist upon a pre-interview meeting whenever possible.

Once in the studio and live on air you are on your own. Relax, be yourself. Unless you have agreed to a controversial interview, the interviewer is on your side, and as keen for the interview to be as successful as you would wish it to be. Enjoy the moment.

Recorded interviews, on the other hand, are much more relaxed affairs. Cutting and splicing were invented for just such occasions. You will not be on your guard all the time to make sure that you do not say 'errum' or any other meaningless words that you may use habitually.

Visits by television crews to your workshop can be exciting, very disruptive and time consuming events. Which channel, programme and the length of time to be devoted to your feature will depend on the size of the camera crew sent. With all the bodies and lights it can get very cosy in a small studio/workshop. There will as before be the informal chat where they will explain to you what it is about your work that they wish to capture. Feel free at this time to make suggestions. Always remember that these people, with the best intention in the world, cannot be as familiar with the many aspects of your work as you are. It will not be through stupidity that they omit something obvious, but through lack of knowledge.

Apart from the occasional difficult experience, I have always found the people that one meets and works with in the media extremely helpful. They will know from experience what will and will not work in their field as you do in your own. Respect their views, work with them, and you will find that not only have you made a good item that will give you the publicity you sought with your press release, but in years to come, they will recognise and read your press releases and, when it is appropriate, they will come to you and ask 'What's new?' 'Are you doing anything interesting that we can use?'

It goes without saying – having made these good and useful contacts – *Put them on your index file.*

CHAPTER FIFTEEN

Public Relations

Public Relations (P.R.) is building a relationship with the public, ie. the art of putting your name in front of the public in a positive way as often is possible. In Chapter 14 we discuss the subjects for press releases that would occur naturally as part of the normal business year, unusual commissions, exhibitions, open weekends, etc., this is the essence of public relations. You may consider that exhibitions and open weekends are prime selling occasions, that an unusual commission is all part of a day's work, but they are also excellent opportunities to use to get your name in the public eye. The continual chip, chipping that you do on the awareness of the general public will all help to increase their knowledge of you and enhance your reputation. This in the long run will result in new clients, increased confidence to commission for those prospective clients who are unsure, and positive reinforcement of their decision to buy for existing customers.

Big companies pay vast sums of money to better their reputations in the market place. Firms and organisations that have a monopoly on the markets they supply indulge in public relations to improve their image, maybe as environmentalists or perhaps they are trying to overcome some bad publicity they have received in the recent past. We hear much of the British royal family trying to improve their image with some good P.R.; even politicians now resort to consulting P.R. firms. If these doyens of society with the experts they have on hand to advise them feel the need for P.R. then who are we to fly in the face of such auspicious reasoning?

Apart from the opportunities resulting from the daily running of the business there will always be occasions and ideas, some contrived, that will serve as good public relations exercises. It is knowing which to develop, accept or reject. You must, of course, always be level-headed in your decisions and objectively consider if the concept, event, audience and venue will be correct, and if there will be a possibility of extra publicity from the media.

Most of these activities are time consuming and the results will not be immediately apparent or quantifiable, so it is difficult to weigh the advantages and disadvantages and then decide. Target carefully where and to whom you perform these adventures into the P.R. field. Be absolutely callous, it is your time you are giving, give it where it will most benefit you. Never forget with any of these ventures that they are only worth doing if you do them properly, with the degree of quality and competence you wish people to perceive is present in your work. Do not get involved with an event which you see as denigrating or trivialising your work. Whilst it is admirable to do things for charity, do not allow your work to be badly displayed, or give a talk or a demonstration where the facilities are inadequate and your professionalism and expertise will be overshadowed by inefficiency and excessive amateurism. It would be wiser to give a donation or some of your time lending a hand with the mundane organising of such events if you feel that the cause is worthy.

It is very easy to get yourself known for giving talks and slide shows 'on the circuit', that is, to all the Probus Clubs, W.I groups, Friends of (the local) Museum, etc, within a reasonable travelling distance from home. The reference library will be able to supply names and addresses to contact within each of these organisations, who always seem to be looking for new and interesting speakers and slide shows. It is unusual for the fee to be very high or to do more than pay for the petrol and a drink on the way home, but it is very difficult to know where the contacts may lead, and sometimes the fee is sufficient to make the whole exercise worthwhile without any spin-off.

The organiser will advise on the duration of the talk, tell you what facilities they have available and ask what else may be required. Be sure before you offer your service that you are able to talk, or that your photographs are of a quality to give a good slide show. It is imperative that several rehearsals are held before the very first session. Once that has been undertaken your confidence will grow, unless it really is not for you, you will begin to relax and your talking ability will improve with every session. Up-date your slides at every opportunity, and as giving talks becomes a regular part of your working life you may consider obtaining your own projector, screen, pointer, etc. to avoid any possible mishaps.

Demonstrating your craft is not for the feint-hearted, but if you can do it and the venue is suitable then it can attract a lot of attention. This is something you could combine with an open weekend at your own studio/workshop, people love to watch the true craftsman at work. Always make a list of your requirements if you are doing this away from home and double check your list before you leave, it is so easy to leave an essential item on the workbench. This is an ideal situation for a press release. If you are part of a big event the organisers usually see to the media, but sometimes they require input from the participants. Always enquire, and be prepared with a few photographs and a short write-up about yourself and your work. Use an A4 sheet of paper, wide margins, double line spaced and your name at the top of the page.

When you talk, demonstrate, display your work, take part in craft fairs, receive visitors at your showroom or workshop, etc. you should always have something available to give away to people as a reminder of your work. This can be a postcard, sales literature, a recent exhibition catalogue, or a business card. Do not leave them in piles on your display as this may detract from the layout of the work, but one or two strategically placed will encourage visitors to request them. Not only will this give you an opportunity to enter into a discussion if that seems appropriate, but it will deter the paperwork collectors from gathering as they pass.

Depending on your particular craft it may be possible to produce a small quality item to give away, items that will work in your absence as a reminder and a sample of your work. It would be easy to render this idea useless by trivialising your craft, but careful thought and discrete distribution will work in your favour. The item should, of course, bear your name or logo and be something used or seen regularly, leather key fobs, ceramic napkin rings, wooden letter openers, etc.

If your work is featured in a book or magazine and the article contains a piece belonging to one of your clients it is in the interest of good customer relations to ensure that they receive a copy. Sometimes, you may feel that these forays into public relations are costly, especially if the budget is a little tight and you are off to the newsagents to buy six copies of a magazine, six envelopes and six stamps. You must consider this action in a more constructive manner, initially that of common courtesy to your client and secondly as a cold-blooded sales ploy of putting your name on his breakfast table in a very positive way.

Christmas and birthday cards are a very pleasant way of saying hello to your clients and giving them a gentle reminder of your existence. Birthdays are not very easy to collect, asking is not terribly subtle, but it is possible to be attentive and write down any that you discover. This is easier than at first it appears. Many items are bought as presents or to celebrate an occasion and as these are not secrets they will be openly discussed in front of you; all you have to do is remember to put it in your diary and then send a suitable greetings card.

Having your own Christmas cards printed is expensive, but it does have the advantage of carrying your own particular message, name and address, as well as a festive, or otherwise, illustration of work. An alternative is to choose a card and a greeting and have your name and address printed inside. If you buy standard cards from the normal retailers, as with both of the other methods, select a good quality card with the minimum of greeting. Merry Christmas and a Happy New Year are adequate. Then you must be sure to sign your card, it is ill-mannered to send an unsigned card. If you have bought ready made cards you may feel it necessary to sign with your full name, but this will not always be necessary if you have your name and address printed inside. Hand write the envelopes, or type them, no computer labels. Birthday cards should also be chosen for their simple 'Happy Birthday' message, nothing flowery or embarrassing, this could render the thought counter productive.

There are other more contrived methods of seeking good P.R. You could sponsor a local event, give an annual cup with your name on it. This would attract a little local media attention as well as promoting yourself amongst the people directly concerned with the activity. If you felt you could afford to sponsor a trophy for a local event, then for your purposes the local tennis or squash club may well have a wealthier clientele than the local boys' football club, or vice versa. Which one would have the most kudos attached to it? Do your research well first. True, secretive altruism is the reserve of the successful, the rich and private conscience, not to be confused with business.

Giving away actual pieces of your work to prominent people or organisations in the hope of publicity, and/or other more tangible benefits will entirely depend on what you make, and the cost of the item to you in time and money. If you make mugs, and give six to the mayor to celebrate his coming to office, you will probably get a photo in the local paper. If you can secure a visit to your workshop by the mayor to collect them, then you will almost certainly get coverage in the local paper, if not a piece on the local television news. Your six mugs will have been well spent. But if you make more expensive items ideas like this must be more carefully thought out, if given any credence at all. If you are going to do something like this it would be prudent to write your own press release, rather than rely on the press finding out by a more circuitous route. When writing the press release, using who, what, where, when and why, make sure you have a suitable reason for the why question. If it is an obvious publicity stunt, it probably will not work, but if you have heard that the mayor likes his tea in a mug and there are only teacups available in the mayor's parlour then what better reason could you ask for. You have successfully done your research and exploited an opportunity to good effect.

*   *   *   *

Working on the presumption that your work is sound – that is, well designed and well made – this book has set out the basic principles and practices of marketing, promotion and public relations which should stand you in good stead when approaching the selling aspect of your trade. What has been written here has been practised first hand over a good number of years in my own business. Marketing and promotion are skills to be learnt and developed and will bring you the success which your artistic endeavours deserve.

Bibliography

Michael Bland – Be your own P.R. Man, A pubic relations guide for the small business man – Kogan Page.

Edward De Bono – Six Thinking Hats – Penguin Books.

James Borg – The Inner Game of Selling Yourself – Mandarin.

David Butler – Making Ways, The Visual Artists' Guide to Surviving and Thriving – Artists Newsletter Publications.

Dale Carnegie – How to Win Friends and Influence People – World's Work Ltd.

Elwood N. Chapman – How to Develop a Positive Attitude – Kogan Page.

Colin Coulson-Thomas – Public Relations, A Practical Guide – Macdonald & Evans.

John Courtis – Marketing Services, A Practical Guide – Kogan Page.

Crafts Council – Running a Workshop – Crafts Council.

Philip B. Crosby – Running Things, The Art of Making Things Happen – McGraw-Hill.

John Crowe & James Stokes – Art, Design & Craft, A Manual for Business Success – Edward Arnold.

Rodney Dale – The Sinclair Story – Duckworth.

Philippa Davies – Your Total Image, How to Communicate Success – Piatkus.

Peter F. Drucker – Managing for Results – Pan Books.

Debbie Duffin – Organising Your Own Exhibition, A Guide For Artists – ACME.

Edwin B. Feldman, P.E. – How to use your time to get things done – Frederick Fell Publishers Inc.

Patricia Garnier – Career in Crafts – Kogan Page

John Harvey Jones – Making it Happen, Reflections on Leadership – Fontana/ Collins.

Marion E. Haynes – Make Every Minute Count – Kogan Page.

Sarah Hoskins – Working for Yourself in the Arts and Crafts – Kogan Page.

Greville Janner – Janner on Presentation – Business Books.

Susan Jones – Directory of Exhibition Spaces – Artists Newsletter Publications.

Victor Kiam – Going For It, How to Succeed as an Entrepreneur – Fontana/ Collins

Maxwell Maltz – Psycho-Cybernetics, A New Technique for using your Subconcious Power – Wilshire Book Company.

Robert S. L. Nathan – Selling Crafts – David & Charles.

Norman Vincent Peale – The Power of Positive Thinking, A Practical Guide to Mastering the Problems of Everyday Living – World's Work Ltd.

Thomas J. Peters & Robert H. Waterman Jr. – In Search of Excellence – Harper Collins

Rosemary Pettit – The Craft Business – Pitman Publishing.

Richard D. Smith & Ginger Dick – Getting Sales, A practical guide to getting more sales for your business – Kogan Page.

Ben Sweetland – Grow Rich While You Sleep – Thorsons.

Stuart Turner – Thorsons Guide to Public Relations, How to give any project the best chance of success – Thorsons.

Stuart Turner – Practical Sponsorship – Kogan Page.

Publications from Stobart Davies Ltd

Fundamentals of Figure Carving *Ian Norbury*—A highly visual study, illustrated with over 300 superb drawings and photographs of carving the human figure in wood.

Beyond Basic Turning *Jack Cox*—This wood turning book covers off-centre, coopered, laminated and segmented work. Very detailed with over 300 illustrations and explicit instructions to help produce fine turned work.

The Book of Boxes *Andrew Crawford*—A complete practical guide to box making and box design. Clear step-by-step drawings and photographs in full colour throughout.

World Woods in Colour *William Lincoln*—275 commercial world timbers in full colour, describing general characteristics, properties and uses table. 300 pages.

The Complete Manual of Wood Finishing *Frederick Oughton*—An encyclopaedic work on the traditional craft of wood finishing. 288pp illustrated. Highly detailed and extensive in scope.

Techniques of Creative Woodcarving *Ian Norbury*—A complete work with emphasis on the practical side of figure carving. 160pp 200 illustrations.

British Craftmanship in Wood *Betty Norbury*—Comprehensive coverage of almost 200 individual craftsmens' work, including 450 examples of the finest handmade woodwork of the twentieth century.

What Wood is That? *Herbert L Edlin*—A unique book which contains a collection of 40 wood veneer samples in a folding wallet. The samples are described throughout the book in terms of fourteen key characteristics.

Mouldings & Turned Woodwork of the 16th, 17th & 18th Centuries *T Small & C Woodbridge*—A rich source of ideas and applications of turned woodwork and mouldings presented in full-size details and sections.

Making Wooden Clock Cases *Tim & Peter Ashby*—Presenting complete measured drawings and detailed plans for 20 clocks for the craftsman to make. Includes detailed illustrations and both metric and imperial measurements. A full range of suppliers for clock components completes the book.

Creative Woodturning *Dale L Nish*—Step by step instructions for the woodturner. 630 photographs. 256pp., 8 in colour.

The Marquetry Manual *William Lincoln*—This state-of-the -art publication incorporates all the traditional ideas and practices for marquetarians as well as all the current thinking, and a selection of some of the greatest marquetry pictures. 272 pages, 400 illustrations.

Modern Practical Joinery *George Ellis*—This vast coverage of internal joinery includes windows, doors, stairs, handrails, mouldings, shopfitting and showcase work, all clearly detailed and illustrated with hundreds of line drawings. Nearly 500 pages and 27 chapters.

The Construction of Period Country Furniture *V J Taylor*—28 designs of period furniture to make. Includes complete constructional details and plans. 192pp.

Artistic Woodturning *Dale L Nish*—Step by step instructions with more than 700 photographs including 39 in full colour. 264pp.

Relief Woodcarving and Lettering *Ian Norbury*—Caters for all levels of ability from beginners onwards, exploring the fields of low and high relief carving through a series of graded projects. 157pages, fully illustrated.

The Complete Manual of Wood Veneering *William Lincoln*—Extensive coverage of all the techniques used in furniture and craftwork. 400 pages. Fully illustrated.

Reproducing Antique Furniture *F Gottshall*—Contains 37 projects each with highly detailed working drawings. 240 pages—over 600 illustrations.

Cabinetmaking—The Professional Approach *Alan Peters*—A major work covering all aspects of working as a designer and cabinetmaker. 200 pages—8 in colour.

Projects for Creative Woodcarving *Ian Norbury*—Over 50 projects to inspire the woodcarver. Beautifully illustrated.

Wood Machining *Nigel Voisey*—A fresh approach to *the* most important area of workshop practice—safety. 144pp with photographs and line drawings.

Spindle Moulder Handbook *Eric Stephenson*—Covers all aspects of this essential woodworking machine from spindle speeds to grinding and profiling. 200 pages—430 photos and line drawings.

Making Early Stringed Instruments *Ronald Zachary Taylor*—A complete guide containing measured drawings, diagrams, construction notes and chapters on materials and tools needed for eight early musical stringed instruments. Instruments include a Classic Guitar, Dulcimer, Gothic Harp and many others.

Machine Woodworking Technology for Hand Woodworkers *F E Sherlock*—Covers virtually all the machines and associated technology that the hand woodworker is likely to encounter. 214 pages, illustrated throughout.